An Observational Cross Sectional Study on Pulmonary Function, Oxidative Stress, Inflammatory Biomarkers and Genotoxicity among Workers in Silver Jewellery Units, Coimbatore

Author

Dr K.V. SHALINI

Assistant Professor

Department of Biochemistry, Biotechnology and Bioinformatics

Avinashilingam Institute for Home Science and Higher Education for Women

SHANLAX PUBLICATIONS

SHANLAX #SINCE1990

Title: AN OBSERVATIONAL CROSS SECTIONAL STUDY ON PULMONARY FUNCTION, OXIDATIVE STRESS, INFLAMMATORY BIOMARKERS AND GENOTOXICITY AMONG WORKERS IN SILVER JEWELLERY UNITS, COIMBATORE

Author's Name: Dr K.V. Shalini

Published by: Shanlax Publications,
Vasantha Nagar, Madurai - 625003,
Tamil Nadu, India

Publisher's Address: 61, 66 T.P.K. Main Road,
Vasantha Nagar, Madurai - 625003,
Tamil Nadu, India

Printer's Details: Shanlax Press, 66 T.P.K. Main Road,
Vasantha Nagar, Madurai - 625003,
Tamil Nadu, India

Edition Details (I,II,III): I

ISBN: 978-93-93737-42-7

Month & Year: January, 2022

Pages: 118

Price: ₹240 /-

ACKNOWLEDGEMENT

This book is based on research conducted on the occupational health hazards of the silver jewellery workers between 2016 to 2019. There are many people to whom I am grateful to and fears that the space is not enough to thank them all. First of all, I wish to express my gratitude to **God Almighty**, whose constant presence was a guiding light throughout the course of my research. I am grateful for number of friends and family members in encouraging me to start the work, preserve with it and finally to publish it.

This minor research project was obtained at Rathnavel subramaniam College of Arts and Science, Sulur, Coimbatore and completed successfully funded by University Grant Commission (UGC).I gratefully acknowledge the funding sources UGC that supported the research expenses. I thank Dr. M.P Ayyappadas , Vice principal, Head Department of Biotechnology and Dr. S. Sivakumar, Principal, Rathnavelsubramaniam College of Arts and Science, Sulur, Coimbatore for extending all possible help towards the completion of the study.

I articulate my deep felt thanks to post graduate **students** especially S.Arunkumar and G.Arunkumar of the Department of Biotechnology, Rathnavel subramaniam College of Arts and Science, Sulur, Coimbatore who were always helpful, considerate and supportive for the sample collection.

I cannot find words to thank my family for shouldering me during days when nothing seemed right. The mere mention of their names wouldn't do justice to the care and support they gave. I am highly indebted to my **mother**, **father**, **husband and child** for their prayers, motivation, support, and encouragement in making this study a reality. They all kept me going and this book would not have been possible without them.

CONTENTS

AN OBSERVATIONAL CROSS SECTIONAL STUDY ON PULMONARY FUNCTION, OXIDATIVE STRESS, INFLAMMATORY BIOMARKERS AND GENOTOXICITY AMONG WORKERS IN SILVER JEWELLERY UNITS, COIMBATORE

1

Introduction

Metal pollution is a major public health problem in developing countries. Metal pollution affects the physical and mental development of an individual leading to decreased work capacity that in turn affects the development of a country. The impact of environmental exposure to toxic metals on human health has been discussed in numerous publications over the past 20 years (Singh et al.,2007).

Indoor air pollution is fast growing global issue, as it poses a major risk to human health. In jewellery making units, the workers work in small dingy rooms filled with smoke from the acid that is used during refining and polishing processes (Lansdown2002).

The manufacturing of silver jewellery consists of large number of stages starting with refining of silver before proceeding to shouldering, crafting and polishing. The units engaged in refining and polishing operations use nitric acid and sulphuric acid. These hazardous chemical semit fumes and dusts during jewellery making processes (Lansdown2002).

Acute and chronic health effects have been encountered in personnel's who are working in jewellery making industries. Chronic exposure to airborne particles in this units leads to various respiratory ailments. Exposure to airborne particles may cause external, internal and adverse health effects which include allergic, mucosal and non respiratory effects, dermatitis and cancer (Watanabe,2004;Devietal.,2012).

Silver (Ag) occurs naturally in its pure form. It has been valued as a precious metal used to make ornaments, tablewares, utensils, and currency coins (Chenetal., 2008; Panyala et al., 2008). It is also used industrially in electrical conductors, mirrors, and catalysis of chemical reactions. Its compounds are used in photographic film and are also used as dental alloys, disinfectants, and microbicides (Drake and Hazelwood, 2005).

It has been known that Ag-based compounds are useful in a wide range of bactericidal applications (Sivakumar et al., 2012). Important sources of atmospheric Ag from human activities include steel refining, fossil-fuel combustion, cement manufactures, processing of ores, cloud seeding, and municipal waste incineration. Recent studies confirm that Ag in its metallic state is inert but it gets ionized when it reacts with moisture and body fluids. The ionized Ag is highly reactive, as it binds to tissue proteins and brings structural changes in the bacterial cell wall and nuclear membrane leading to cell distortion and death. Ag ions react rapidly with prokaryotic cell walls, whereas the membranes of eukaryotic cells strongly resist the effect of Ag Lansdown 2002; Castellano et al., 2007).

However, some of the recent studies also indicated that Ag and Ag compounds show unacceptable toxic effect on human health and the environment. The chronic exposure to

Ag causes adverse effects such as permanent bluish-gray discoloration of the skin (argyria) and eyes (argyrosis) (Gulbranson et al., 2000). Exposure to soluble Ag compounds may produce other toxic effects such as liver and kidney damage, irritation of the eyes, skin, respiratory and intestinal tract, and changes to blood cells. The normal concentrations of Ag in human tissues are very low. If there is an overexposure, it can be accumulated in mucous membranes, corneas, nails, and spleen (Sue et al.,2001).

According to Xiaetal., Agnano particles (AgNPs) can attach to different tissues and cause potential toxic effects, namely, producing reactive oxygen species and cell activation (Xia et al., 2006). It is more and tissues and gradually lead to cell death. Drake and Hazel wood revealed that skin, eyes, brain, liver, kidneys, spleen, and bone arrow are the principle target tissues for Ag deposition following systemic absorption. Sueetal. reported that the over exposure to Ag can cause accumulation of the Ag ions in the skin, blood, liver, spleen, corneas, mucous membranes, kidneys, hair, gingival, and nails (Sue et al.,2001).

Ag is absorbed into cultured cells by a pinocytic mechanism as in bacteria and fungi which can be interacted with cytoplasmic proteins leading to cell death. According to Arora et al., cultured cells exposed to Ag particles at 6.25-50 µg/mL showed altered cell shape, evidence of oxidative stress, and increased lipid per oxidation.

The Center for Disease Control, National Institute of Occupational Safety and Health, USA recommends performing a complete blood count as an investigation measure among individuals exposed to pollutants of work place environment. Jewellery industries also emits pollutants in regular basis during the manufacturing process. Hence a complete blood count was carried out in peripheral venous blood of the participants.

The pulmonary function test is a significant measure to evaluate effectiveness of respiratory function. These tests are imperative for clinical diagnostic, prognostic value and research purpose too. It is clearly known that pulmonary function test has been useful tool for early detection of pulmonary ailments in patients considering to being normal in accordance with radio logical and clinical examination. Spirometry is a readily available tool to detect lung function abnormalities at an early stage.

It plays a significant role in an industrial respiratory health observation program. It helps health professionals to determine a specific pattern of pulmonary ailments and assists to evaluate the efficiency of measures employed to protect the individual worker. Spirometric (Vitalograph) results of exposed group workers can be assessed in order to know potential occupational hazards (Kim et al., 2008).

Air pollutants induce oxidative stress in the lung and cause chronic respiratory tract and systemic inflammation. Oxidative stress is the imbalance between the production of oxidants and the body's ability to detoxify the reactive intermediates or repair the resulting damage. Oxidant generation is part of the normal cellular metabolism and is critical for cell homeostasis. Inflammatory cells such as macrophages, neutrophils and eosinophils are the most important endogenous generators of oxidants (Bhattacharyya et al., 2010).

Exposure to genotoxic agents in occupational settings is often associated with an elevated risk for DNA damage. Most exposures in an occupational setting are chronic or repeated and the induced DNA damage might be expected to be elevated above baseline levels (Garaj-Vrhovac and Kopjar, 2009). The comet assay or single cell gele lector phoresis is a simple and responsive method for studying DNA damage, and a useful tool for detection of genetic damage at the individual cell level (Olive and Bantah2006).

Ambient air quality will be monitored to assess the pollutant levels in silver jewellery units. The quality of indoor air inside offices and workplaces is important not only for workers comfort but also for their health. Poor in door air quality (IAQ) has been coupled to symptoms include fatigue, headaches, trouble concentrating and irritation of the eyes, nose, throat and lungs. Moreover, some specific diseases have been associated to definite air contaminants or indoor environments. In addition, some exposures do not cause immediate symptoms but can lead to cancer after many years. Hence it is significant to evaluate the indoor air quality at work place environment.

The objective of the present study was to assess the impact of pollutants on the health of silver jewellery workers who are exposed to toxic pollutants in their work place. Selected haematological, biochemical parameters and inflammatory markers in blood, serum and plasma were estimated and pulmonary function tests were performed in them to assess the toxicity caused due to exposure to high levels of pollutants in their work place and thereby to assess their risk for the development of health hazards. Air quality was assessed in silver jewellery units to validate the results.

Objectives

- To assess the pulmonary function among workers in jewellery units
- To estimate the levels of antioxidants and inflammatory markers in the collected samples among workers in jewellery units
- To investigate the genotoxicity of selected jewellery unit workers by comet assay
- To assess the ambient air quality in jewellery units

EXPERIMENTAL PROCEDURE 2

The experimental procedure pertaining to the study on **"An Observational Cross Sectional Study on Pulmonary Function, Oxidative Stress, Inflammatory Biomarkers and Genotoxicity among Workers in Silver Jewellery Units, Coimbatore** is discussed under the following headings:

2.1 SELECTION OF THE PARTICIPANTS OF THE STUDY
2.2 ELICITING INFORMATION FROM THE SELECTEDPARTICIPANTS
2.3 ANALYSIS OF HEMATOLOGICAL INDICES OF SELECTEDPARTICIPANTS
2.4 EVALUATION OF BIOCHEMICALMARKERS
2.5 ANALYSIS OF INFLAMMATORYBIOMARKERS
2.6 SPIROMETRYANALYSIS
2.7 ENOTOXICITYASSESSMENT
2.8 AMBIENT AIR QUALITY IN JEWELLERYUNITS
2.9 STATISTICAL ANALYSIS

2.1 SELECTION OF THE PARTICIPANTS OF THE STUDY

Studied Population

A cross-sectional study was conducted in the silver jewellery making units located in Coimbatore, Tamil Nadu. A total of 159 silver jewellery unit individuals aged 25-55 years who have residing and working in Coimbatore for many years and have been working in these units were asked to participate in the study in which 148 individuals agreed to do so. This study was approved by the Human Ethical Committee (HEC.2017.16) of Avinashilingam Institute for Home Science and Higher Education for Women, Coimbatore.

Fig : 1Selection of Jewellery Unit Workers for the Study

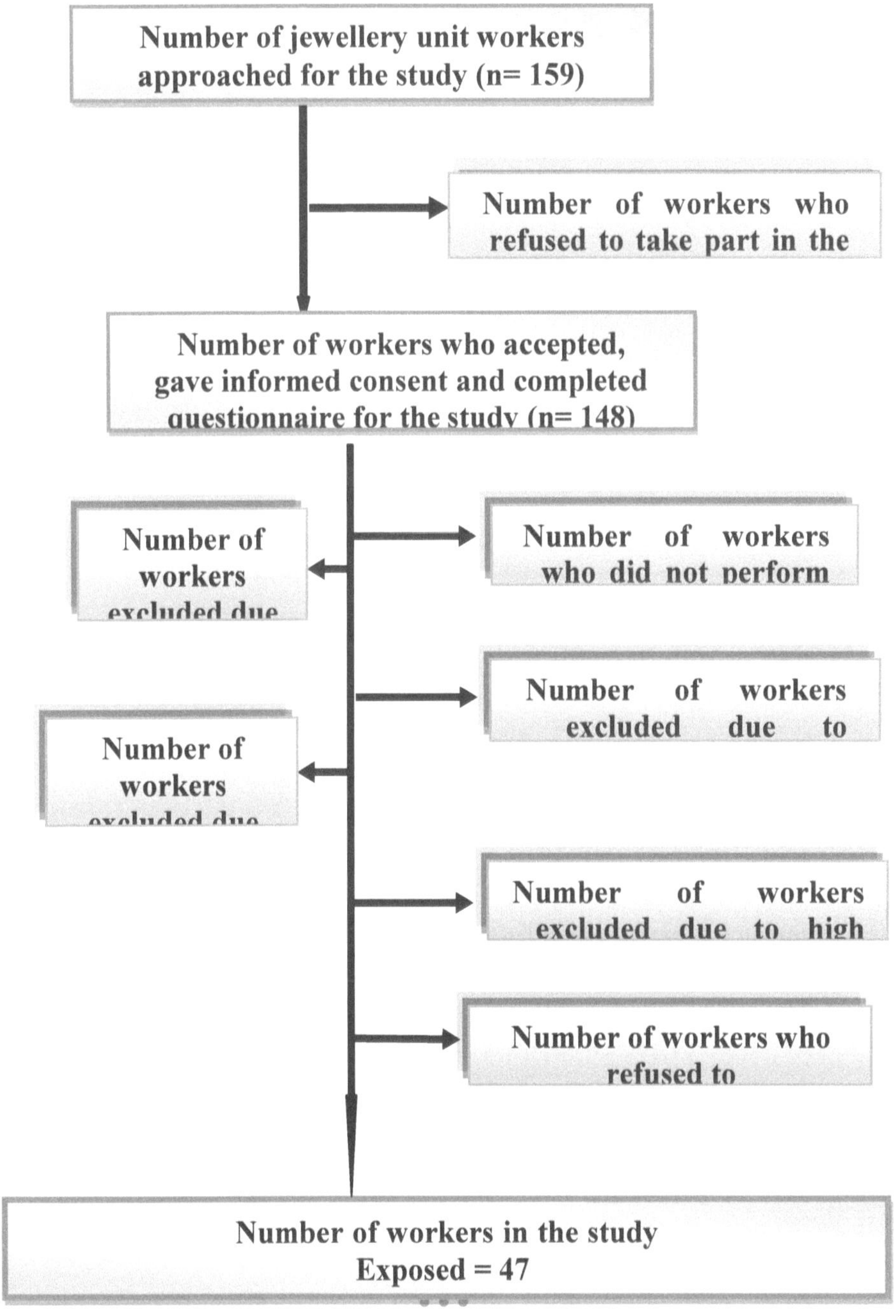

These 148 jewellery unit workers were considered as "exposed group" and control group (unexposed to airborne particles of jewellery units) comprised of 45 individuals who living in the same area with no relation to making of silver jewellery considered as "control group". The demographic and socioeconomic statuses (age, height weight, smoking, and alcoholic habits) were matched between the exposed and control groups.

An in-person survey was carried out for both control and exposed group participants. The study comprised inclusion and exclusion criteria in which workers with minimum 3 year of exposure were included and those with known history of diabetes mellitus, liver diseases, blood transfusion, and any other pathological conditions were excluded from the study.

Each study participant received a questionnaire and was orally explained in local language for illiterate, including questions about employment, residences, smoking, and food habits as well as medical history, especially regarding diabetes and liver diseases. Informed consent was obtained from control and exposed group participants, based on their concern they were included for the study (Appendix1).

2.2 ELICITING INFORMATION FROM THE SELECTEDPARTICIPANTS

Sample Collection and Specimen Preparation

Peripheral venous blood samples (5 ml) were collected from the subjects. All samples for serum (Vacutainers - AcCuvet - PLUS with clot activator) were centrifuged at 3000 rpm at 4°C for 10 minutes. The samples were aliquoted into labeled cryovials and stored at - 20°C for further analysis. Whole blood samples were used for hematological analysis. Fresh blood samples were preserved in ice bags during the collection of samples. Plasma samples were used for the analysis of inflammatory markers.

Based on the inclusion and exclusion criteria 47 exposed and 45 control group participants were selected and spirometric analysis was performed. Workers who have high levels of inflammation biomarkers in the exposed groups (n = 3) and normal controls (n = 3) were selected based on their consent. 1 ml of blood was collected and genotoxicity assay was performed.

Whole blood samples were taken for haematological analysis and serum samples were diluted three-fold with double-distilled water before assay of flame atomic absorption spectroscopy (FAAS).

Height and weight were measured by standard method. Systolic and diastolic blood pressure was measured using Omron Blood Pressure Monitor: HEM 7112. The blood pressure was expressed in mmHg. Analytical methods Serum Ag concentration was determined by FAAS (SHIMADZU, AA7000) and hematological indices were measured on automated 3-part hematology analyzer, Sysmex KX-21. Appendix 2

The spirometry (PC based Helios 401) analysis includes assessment of Vital Capacity (VC), Forced Vital Capacity (FVC), Forced Expiratory Volume in 1 second (FEV1), Forced Expiratory Volume in 6 seconds (FEV6), FEV1/FVC (FEV1 Ratio), Peak Expiratory Flow (PEF), Forced Expiratory Flow 25% - 75% (F25-75), Forced Expiratory Flow 25 % (FEF25), Forced Expiratory Flow 50% (FEF50), Forced Expiratory Flow 75% (FEF75), Peak Inspiratory Flow (PIF) and Maximal Voluntary Ventilation Indirect (MVVInd).

Enzymic and non-enzymic antioxidants include Catalase, superoxide dismutase, glutathione peroxidise, glutathione-S-transferase, vitamin A, vitamin C, vitamin E and reduced glutathione levels were assessed in the collected serum sample. Biochemical parameters such as albumin, total protein, glucose, lipid peroxidation were estimated in the serum sample.

Collection of Demographic Data

Demographics are the quantifiable statistics of a population. It includes age, ethnicity, education, general health details and professional status.

Cigarettes carry serious health risks, which are more prevalent than in other to bacco products (Zhuetal.,2007). The resulting use of tobacco is the single greatest cause of preventable death globally (World Health Organization,2008).

Smoking may lead to diseases which most commonly affects the heart, liver and lungs. It is a major risk factor for heart attacks, strokes, chronic obstructive pulmonary disease (COPD) including emphysema and chronic bronchitis. Cigarette smoking may be a factor that contributes to the occurrence of cancer particularly in lung, mouth, pancreatic and liver. It also causes peripheral vascular disease and hypertension (Centers for Disease Control and Prevention, 2007).

Alcohol consumption also causes major health problems, including cirrhosis of the liver, depression, seizures, gout, high blood pressure, nerve damage, anemia and cardiovascular disease. These two factors may influence the result of the present study. Hence in the present study smoking and history of alcohol consumption were recorded among the workers.

Smoking habits of the selected participants (current smokers) was expressed in pack years which is calculated in terms of number of pack years = (number of cigarettes smoked per day × number of years smoked) /20; 20= number of cigarette in a pack. Alcohol consumption of the selected participants was stated in units/week (1 unit = 10 ml).

2.3 ANALYSIS OF HEMATOLOGICAL INDICES OF SELECTED PARTICIPANTS

Assessment of Haematological Indices

Complete blood count (CBC) is a test panel that gives information about the cells in blood (Buttarello and Plebani, 2008). The cells that circulate in the blood stream are generally divided into three types such as white blood cells (leukocytes), red blood cells (erythrocytes) and platelets (thrombocytes). Abnormally high or low counts may indicate the presence of many forms of disease and hence blood counts are amongst the most commonly performed blood tests in medicine, as they can provide an overview of general health status of an individual (Blesi et al.,2011).

CBC was analyzed in the whole blood of the participants in three part hematological analyzer (Sysmax KX-21). It includes Total Leucocytes and Differential Count, Red Blood Count, Hemoglobin Concentration, Hematocrit (HCT), Mean Corpuscular Volume (MCV), Mean Corpuscular Hemoglobin (MCH), Mean Corpuscular Hemoglobin Concentration (MCHC), Platelet Count, Mean Platelet Volume (MPV), Platelet Distribution Width (PDW) and Red Blood Cell Distribution Width (RDW). The detailed procedure for CBC by Sysmax KX-21 is given in Appendix 2.

2.4 EVALUATION OF BIOCHEMICALMARKERS

Estimate the Levels of Serum Silver

Silver ions (Ag^+) strongly increase the production of reactive oxygen species and also induce the oxidative stress (Krott et al., 2009). Hence in the present study serum levels of silver ions was investigated.

The level of serum silver was assessed by flame atomic absorption spectroscopy (SHIMADZU, AA- 7000). Serum silver status might reflect the past and present, acute and chronic silver exposure among the workers. Silver is a xenobiotic element with less recognized trace metal value in the human body.

Estimation of Serum Glucose

Diabetes mellitus (DM) is a group of metabolic diseases characterized by hyperglycemia resulting from defects in insulin secretion, insulin action, or both. Chronic diabetes is associated with long-term damage, dysfunction and failure of various organs, especially the eyes, kidneys, nerves, heart and blood vessels (American Diabetes Association, 2008). Estimation of glucose in blood is an important parameter assessed in the workers to rule out the DM from the study. Random blood glucose was analyzed by using kit (Agappe diagnostics) based on GOD-PAP method (Appendix4)

Estimation of Serum Total Protein

Total protein measurements are used in the diagnosis and treatment of a variety of diseases involving the liver, kidney, or bone marrow, as well as other metabolic or nutritional disorders (NIOSH. 2003). Serum protein level was estimated by a kit based on biuret method (Appendix 5).

Estimation of Serum Albumin:

Serum albumin levels were estimated by based on bromocresol green method (Appendix 6).

Estimation of Catalase Activity

Cells contain a large number of antioxidants to prevent or repair the damage caused by reactive oxygen species. Catalase converts hydrogen peroxide into water. In this way, two toxic compounds are converted into harmless product. This assay can evaluate the levels of catalase in the tissues and cells. Serum catalase levels were estimated by based on Spectrophotometry method -Luck, 1974 (Appendix 7).

Estimation of Superoxide Dismutase Activity

Superoxide anion (O2-) is a free radical which has a potential to induce oxidative damage. Although they are produced to provide defense, accumulation of the same can induce cellular damage. The estimation of superoxide dismutase enzyme is carried out by Beauchamp and Wheeler and Gregory 1980) method (Appendix 8).

Estimation of Glutathione peroxidase activity

Gpx (Glutathione peroxidase (GPx) is the general name of an enzyme family with peroxidase activity whose main biological role is to protect the organism from oxidative damage. The biochemical function of glutathione peroxidase is to reduce lipid hydroperoxides to their corresponding alcohols and to reduce free hydrogen peroxide to water. Serum glutathione peroxidase activity was estimated spectro photometrically by Rotruck et al., 1973) (Appendix9).

Estimation of Glutathione -S- transferase activity

Glutathioneis capable of preventing damage to important cellular components caused by reactive oxygen species such as free radicals, peroxides, lipid peroxides, and heavy metals. The estimation of glutathione-s-transferase activity is carried out by Spectro photometry method (Habig et al., 1974) (Appendix10).

Estimation of Vitamin A

The four fat soluble vitamins (A,D,E,K) themselves are chemically and biochemically distinct and rarely share common biological dynamics. Vitamin A and E are not biochemically connected, but it is expected to measure them together as their levels may both be compromised in disease of fat malabsorption. Overall, the primary reason for the measurement of vitamin A is to avoid consequences of deficiency or to confirm disease state. The estimation of vitamin A is carried out by Spectro photometry method (Bayfield and Cole, 1980) (Appendix11).

Estimation of Vitamin C

The primary reason for the measurement of vitamin A is to avoid consequences of deficiency or to confirm disease state. The estimation of vitamin C is carried out by Spectro photometry method (Omaye et al., 1979). (Appendix 12).

Estimation of Lipid Per oxidation

Oxidative stress reflects an imbalance between the systemic manifestation of reactive oxygen species and the levels of antioxidant defense system. In humans, oxidative stress is thought to be involved in the development of cancer, Parkinson's disease, atherosclerosis, heart failure and myocardial infarction (Devasagayam, 2004). The oxidative damage is tested by the increase in lipid per oxidation formation.

Among the cellular molecules, lipids contain more than one double bond susceptible to action of free radicals. The resulting reaction is known as lipid per oxidation which produces a large number of by products being studied in relation to diseases. These by products can be measured by the estimation of aldehyde products using thiobarbituric acid (Devasagayam, 2003). Heavy metals induce an increased production of malondialdehyde (MDA), an indicator of lipid per oxidation and whole body free radical activity (Flora et al., 2008). High levels of lipid peroxides are associated with cancer, heart disease, stroke and aging. The details of analysis of this Lipid per oxidation are elaborated in Appendix13.

Estimation of Vitamin E

Vitamin E consists of a group of eight related fat soluble tocopherols and tocotrienols, which have significant antioxidant properties. The highest bioavailability, absorption, and metabolization occur with α-tocopherol. α-tocopherolis considered as the most important lipid soluble antioxid ant since it protects cell membranes from chain reactions caused by radical-induced lipid per oxidation through quenching free radical intermediates (Suzuki and Packer 1993). Hence, levels of α-tocopherol in plasma samples were assessed by HPLC method (Catignani et al., 1983) - (Appendix14).

2.5 ANALYSIS OF INFLAMMATORY BIOMARKERS

Estimation of Clara cell protein

In response to the activity of the environmental pollutants, the lungs have developed their own defense mechanisms, where a major role is played by Claracells (Lakind et al., 2007). These cells secrete Clara cell protein (CC16, CC10 or secreto globin 1A1), an anti- inflammatory protein secreted along the trachea bonchial tree, and the surfactant-associated protein D

(SP-D), which is secreted by the clara cells, alveoli are pi the liumin the deep lung. CC16 is considered the most valuable lung biomarker (Haddam et al., 2009). Determinations of CC16 in blood serum, to which it passively leaks through the bronchoalveo larbarrier, enable its monitoring in the lungs and, indirectly, assessing the condition of the pulmonary epithelial cells (Lakind et al., 2007). To determine the status of lung epithelial cells, an enzyme linked immune sorbent assay kit was used to assess the levels of Clara cell protein in the plasma samples of the subjects (Appendix15).

Estimation of Leukotriene B4 (LTB4):

Leukotrienes are biologically active metabolites that are derived from arachidonic acid through the action of 5- lip oxygenase. Leukotriene B4, a potent chemo attractant for neutrophils, has been involved in the patho physiology of inflammatory airway diseases such as COPD, cystic fibrosis, severe asthma and asthma exacerbation. The quantitative assessment of LTB4 concentrations in biological fluids is essential for establishing the patho physiological role of LTB4 in patients with pulmonary diseases. Identifying abnormal concentrations of LTB4 can she dlight on a specific pathway of inflammation or oxidative stress (Montuschi,2009). An enzyme immune assay kit used to assess the levels of Leukotriene B4 in the plasma of the subjects (Appendix16).

Estimation of Interleukin 8 (IL-8):

IL-8 is a potent neutrophil chemo-attractant playing an important role in inflammation(Pinskyetal.,2009).IL-8 is one of the best biomarkers for lung epithelial barrier injury, inflammation and neutrophil chemotaxis (Ware et al., 2009). Levels of plasma interleukin 8 was estimated by ELISA Kit (Appendix 17).

Estimation of the Activity of Myeloperoxidase (MPO):

Myeloperoxidase (MPO) is an enzyme found in myeloid cells, particularly in neutrophils, and to a lesser extent in monocytes and tissue macrophages. It plays an important role in the host defense against bacteria and viruses. In neutrophils, MPO is located within the primary granules and its concentration is used as an indicator of neutrophil activation and corresponding inflammatory response (Banerjee et al., 2012). MPO is released from activated neutrophils and monocytes during inflammation and has been identified as a novel inflammatory marker (Shah et al., 2008). Myeloperoxidase was estimated in plasma of subjects by ELISA kit -(Appendix18).

2.6 SPIROMETRYANALYSIS

Spirometer

Spirometry was performed by using an electronics pyrometer (PC based Helios 401, India). All respiratory function tests were carried out at a fixed time of the day to minimize the diurnal variation. The apparatus was calibrated daily and operated within the ambient temperature range of 20-25°C. The defined techniques in executing various lung function tests for the present study were based on the operation manual of the instrument with special reference to the official statement of the American Thoracic Society of Standardization of Spirometry. After taking a detailed history and anthropometric data, the subjects were informed about the whole maneuver. The subjects were encouraged to practice this maneuver before doing the pulmonary function test. The test was performed with the subject in the standing position without using a nose clip. The test was repeated three times after adequate rest of 5 min to avoid the exertion. The results were obtained available in the spirometer. These parameters included Forced Vital Capacity (FVC), Forced Expiratory Volume in First Second (FEV1), Forced Expiratory Ratio (FEV1/FVC), Forced Expiratory Flow (FEF25-75%) and Maximum Voluntary Ventilation(MVV).

Fig:2 Spirometer

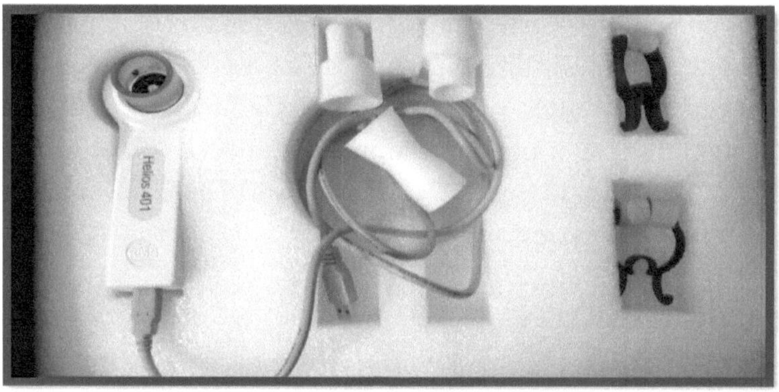

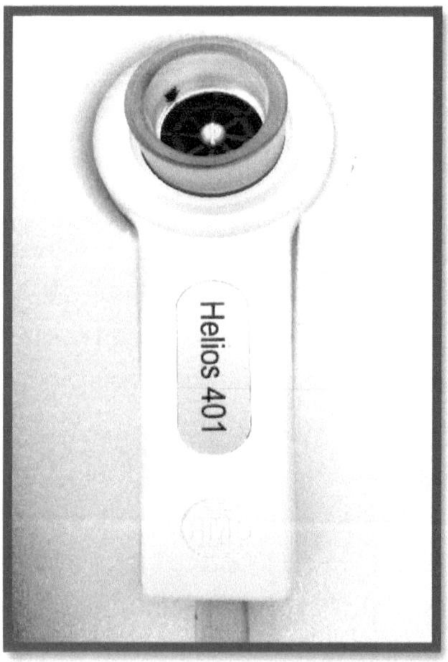

Flow Range	:	-10to+16 liters/sec
Maximum Volume	:	8Liters
Accuracy	:	± 1 % (using a standard 3L calibration syringe)
Transducer	:	Bi-directional turbine cartridge
Turbine sensor	:	Infrared interruption
Flow detection	:	Volume differential

2.7 GENOTOXICITY ASSESSMENT

Occupational exposure to genotoxic agents is often associated with an elevated risk for DNA damage. Most exposures in an occupational setting are chronic or repeated and the induced DNA damage might be expected to be elevated above baseline levels (Garaj-Vrhovac and Kopjar,2009).

Using whole blood samples for the determination of DNA damage is sensible, since valuable time and resources are saved from the separation of peripheral blood lymphocytes (Kayalti et al., 2011). Workers who have high levels of inflammation biomarkers in the exposed groups (n = 3) and normal controls (n = 3) were selected based on their consent. 1 ml of blood was collected and genotoxicity assay was performed. Comat assay was carried out by the protocol of Dhawan and Anderson, 2009 - Appendix 19.

2.8 AMBIENT AIR QUALITY IN JEWELLERY UNITS

Air quality standards are concentrations of pollutants in the work place environment. The criteria are specified for a variety of reasons including for the protection of human health, crops and ecosystem. The sources of air pollutants include vehicles, industries, domestic sources and natural sources. Because of the presence of high amount of air pollutants in the ambient air, the health of the population and property is getting adversely affected. In order to arrest the deterioration in air quality, Govt. of India has enacted Air (Prevention and Control of Pollution) Act in 1981. The responsibility has been further emphasized under Environment (Protection) Act, 1986. It is necessary to assess the present and anticipated air pollution through continuous air quality survey/monitoring programs. Therefore, Central Pollution Control Board had started National Ambient Air Quality Monitoring (NAAQM) Network during 1984 - 85 at national level. The programme was later renamed as National Air Quality Monitoring Programme(NAMP).

Hence, to assess the indoor air quality of the jewellery units in the present study, ambient air quality was monitored at select photocopier units (n=3) during a work day to assess the levels of exposure of jewellery workers to in door air pollutants. The following parameters were assessed in the jewellery units by the methods indicated next to them.

Carbon monoxide(CO) - IS13270:2003
Nitrogen dioxide (NO2) - IS 5182:P6:2006
Ultra fine particular matter(PM2.5) - EPA 40 CFR:P50:L
Volatile organic compounds(VOC) - HSE MDHS 96
Ozone(O3) – IS5182:P9:1974

2.9 STATISTICAL ANALYSIS

SPSS package version 16.0 was used for the statistical analysis of data. The statistically significant level was set at $p<0.05$. Shapiro-Wilk test was carried out to find the normal distribution of the data ($p>0.05$). Student test was conducted and ANOVA was performed for normally distributed data and if the data showed variation at significant level ($p< 0.05$). Mann-Whitney test was done for non - normally distributed data.ChisquaretestandFisher'sexacttestwereconductedforcateg oricalvariables. Spearman's rank correlation was performed to find out association between the parameters.

RESULT AND DISCUSSION 3

Health Status of Workers in Jewellery Units

Silver is the ideal industrial material. It has been used in wide variety of applications such as pharmaceuticals, electrical, chemical catalyst, industrial, printed circuitry, superconductors, electroplating, brazing, soldering, coins, photography, silverware and jewellery (Panyala et al., 2008). A wide variety of uses of silver in industries allows its exposure through various routes of entry into the body. Soluble and insoluble silver compounds have the potential to cause adverse effect to the human health (Weir, 1979).

Silver can gain entry into the body through inhalation, ingestion and dermal absorption of occupational settings. Acute symptoms of over exposure of silver nitrate causes diarrhea, decreased blood pressure, stomach pain and reduced respiration. A chronic symptom of low level exposure to silver salts causes alteration in blood cells and fatty degradation of liver and kidneys (Nordbergetal., 2011).Long term inhalation and ingestion of soluble silver compounds may cause argyria and argyrosis (Gulbranson et al.,2000).

Demographic Profile of the Selected Workers Employed in Jewellery Units

Table 1 and 2 illustrate the profile of selected jewellery unit workers as per the information obtained by administering the questionnaire.

Educational Qualification

Among the jewellery unit workers only 6 were graduates which might point out ignorance of participants about the pollution and toxicity caused by this industry.

Marital Status

Hundred and sixteen were married among the 148 workers of jewellery units. Except 5 out of 116 jewellery unit workers, all others had children with normal behavioral habits. This indicated that there were no toxic effects of silver on reproduction among the jewellery unit workers. Unlike other metals, metallic silver is not toxic to humans and is not known to cause cancer, reproductive or neurological damage and other chronic adverse effects. Prolonged exposure to silver dust or fumes can cause mild effects on human health.

Table 1
Demographic Profile of the Selected Workers Employed in Jewellery Units

Factors	Control group (n= 45)	Jewellery unit workers (n= 148)
Educational qualification		
a) < 5thStandard	8	31
b) 5th-12thStandard	31	98
c) Graduates	6	19
Maritalstatus		
a) Married	33	116
b) Unmarried	12	32
Workexperience		
a) 3-12years	10	37
b) 13-22years	23	71
c) >22years	12	40
Economic background (Income/Month in Rupees)		
a) Up to 5000	11	67
b) 5001 to 8000	24	56
c) 8001 and above	10	25

ButAg2+ (ionized form of silver) is found to inhibit human sperm creatine kinase activity (required for high energy) in a dose dependent manner. Even though it was identified as heavy metal and was correlated with an over all decrease in male fertility, the exact mechanism is not clearly known (Ghaffari and Motlagh,2011).

Work Experience

Based on the duration of the work experience, 148 jewellery unit workers were categorized in to 3-12 years (n = 37), 13-22 years (n = 71) and more than 22 years (n = 40) of exposure in this unit.

Economic Background

Among the exposed group participants, 67 had monthly income of up to Rs. 5000, 56 had Rs. 5001- 8000 and 25 had an income above Rs.8001.

Table2 presents the details of age and alcohol in take among the jewellery unit workers

Table 2
Demographic Profile of the Selected Workers Employed in Jewellery Units

Groups	Age*	Frequency of alcohol consumption /Week*
Control group (n = 45)	35±1.32	9.32±1.22
Exposed group (n =148)	34±1.17	9.48±1.22
p value (>0.05)	0.254	0.511

*= Mean ± Standard deviation
Student t test was conducted

Age

The distribution of age among the control and jewellery unit workers is summarized in table 2. The present study indicated that there was no significant difference ($p>0.05$) in the distribution of age between the control and exposed groups.

Alcohol Consumption

Alcohol consumption and smoking habits are considered as the confounding and environmental factors which might interfere in the findings of the present study. Hence smoking status (current smokers, passive smokers and ex smokers) and alcohol consumption were documented for all the subjects.

The impact of alcohol consumption was found in major diseases such as cancer in nasopharynx, oropharynx, colon, rectum, breast, liver and oesophagus, hypertension and ischaemic heart disease, diabetes mellitus, unipolar depressive disorders, haemorrhagic stroke, epilepsy, cirrhosis of the liver and lower respiratory infections (Rehmetal.,2010). The present study showed that there was no significant difference ($p > 0.05$) among alcoholic intake between control and exposed groups which indicated that alcohol consumption did not confound the study results.

Smoking Habits of Workers Among Jewellery Units Pack Years (Smoking Habit)

Smoking is considered to be a vital factor for many pathological conditions. It influences both innate and adoptive immune responses. It may lead to high levels of numerous pro-inflammatory cytokines, anti-inflammatory cytokines and elevated levels of IgE causing atopic diseases and asthma (Jensen et al., 1988).

Silver acetate chewing gum is used as a smoking deterrent, which may lead to accumulation of silver in skin and cause the development of argyria (Jensen et al., 1988). The present study did not indicate any significant difference ($p>0.05$) in current smoking habit between the control and jewellery unit workers. Current smoking habit of the selected participants was expressed in pack years.

Ex Smokers

Ex smokers include people who have previously been smokers. The present study consisted of 12 members who were former smokers in jewellery units. There was no significant difference ($p>0.05$) observed in the ex-smoking habit of control and exposed group workers of the study.

Passive Smokers

Passive smoking is the inhalation of smoke (second-hand smoke), or environmental tobacco smoke by persons other than active smoker. Passive smoking may cause heart diseases (Wells, 1994), obstructive respiratory disease (Day aletal., 1994), fertility problems and even breast cancer in women (Repace, 1981). There were 32 out of 148 participants as passive smokers among the exposed group of the study. In this study, there was no significant difference ($p > 0.05$) in the passive smoking habit of control and exposed group.

The present study showed that there was no significant difference ($p>0.05$) among smoking habit of current smokers, passive smokers and ex smokers between control and exposed groups which indicated that smoking habit did not confound the study results.

Chewing tobacco users

Eight members of exposed group were found to be chewable tobacco users in the present study. Chewing tobacco seemed to cause minor problems such as tooth stains, gum problems, losing taste for food, bad breath and many health problems. The most serious problems are white patches and sores inside the mouth which leads to cancer (Kademani, 2007). The present study showed that there was no significant difference ($p>0.05$) in the chewing tobacco habit between the control and exposed group workers.

Table 3 presents the details of ex smokers, passive smokers and chewing tobacco users of jewellery unit workers.

Table 3

Smoking Habit of the Jewellery Units Workers

Factors	Control (n=45)	Jewellery unit workers (n=148)	p value ($p < 0.05$)
Pack Years* Ex smokers	0.12±1.15	0.13 ±1.89	0.654
Yes	3	12	
No	42	136	0.321$
Passive smokers			
Yes			
No	13	32	0.758 $
Chewing tobacco users	32	116	
Yes	2	8	
No	43	140	0.127$

* Values are expressed as Mean± Standard deviation Student t test was performed

$ F Values for Chi square test

Besides drug or industrial exposures, silver may being ested with foods (wheat flour, bran and mushroom), milk and water. Few studies indicated that silverproducts have the potential risk for the developing fet us in pregnant women (Landsdown,2010). High concentration of silver exposure was found to cause glomerular damage and proteinuria. Metal fume fever and chemical pneumonitis seemed to arise due to inhaled silver (Sullivan and Krieger, 2001). Topical use of silver nitrate in burns was found to lead to methe moglobinemia (Sharma et al., 2006).

Since none of the workers in the present study consumed any colloidal silver nor silver containing medicines for illness, silver exposure in them might be believed to be mostly due to silver from the jewellery units.

Protective Measures in Use Among Jewellery Unit Workers

Table 4 shows the details of the protective measures regularly used by the jewellery unit workers (n = 148).

Table 4
Protective Measures in Use Among Jewellery Unit Workers (N=148)

Protective measures	Yes (%)	No (%)
Respiratory mask	-	148 (100%)
Gloves	12 (7.6%)	136 (92.4%)
Safety glasses	7 (4.4%)	141 (95.6%)
Chappals	23 (14.6%)	125 (85.4%)
Avoidance of eating during work hours	8 (5.1%)	140 (94.9%)
Avoidance of drinking during working hours	5 (3.2%)	143 (96.8%)
All the above protective measures	-	148(100%)

Prevention of occupational hazards is much more effective and cheaper rather than as control solutions of already existing hazardous situations. The personal protective measures such as air filters, respiratory protective equipments, shoes and gloves reduce the effects of hazardous pollutants to human at work place. Ingestion of hazardous compounds that occurs through drinking and eating in the work place should be forbidden (World Health Organization, 1999). According to Nij et al.(2003), the combined use of more than one protective measure can reduce exposures to acceptable levels of pollutants.

Symptoms Reported by Jewellery Unit Workers

Table 5 features the symptoms reported by selected jewellery unit workers which were elicited by administering questionnaire.

The most prominent symptom seen in exposed group workers was abdominal pain (42%) followed by muscle weakness (32%) among the jewellery unit workers in the present study. Out of 148 jewellery unit workers, 18% people reported eye irritation and throat pain and 2% persons reported wheezing and allergy. Twenty three percent and 16% people informed head ache and dry skin respectively.

Oral consumption of colloidal silver may result in agranulocytosis, hemolysis, pleural edema and coma. Ingestion of large dose of inorganic silver may lead to burning of throat, abdominal pain, diarrhea, vomiting and convulsion as reported by Weir (1979).

None of the jewellery unit workers showed argyria (discoloration of the skin) and argyrosis (discoloration of the eyes) which is a symptom of severe silver toxicity. Forty eight (30%) out of 148 workers were absolutely normal as Sanchez-

Huerta et al. (2003) opined that there is a wide variation in individual susceptibility to silver intoxication. Some individuals have clinical symptoms due to silver exposure at an early stage and may begin at a low dose whereas, in others, symptoms may not appear until high dose. A number of factors influence on metals to produce toxic effect on human body such as solubility, binding ability with protein, metabolism and excretion.

Continuous exposure to silver compounds for prolonged period of time may cause blue-gray pigmentation on skin and body tissues. Exposure to fumes and dust of silver nitrate and silver oxide at high dose may cause lung and throat irritation, breathing problems, vomiting and stomach pain. Skin contact with silver compounds may cause mild allergic reactions such as rashes, redness of skin and swelling as reported by Agency for Toxic Substances and Disease Registry (1990).

Table 5
Symptoms Reported by Jewellery Unit Workers

Symptoms/ History	Exposed (n=148)	Control (n=45)
Throat pain	2	2
Dry Skin	7	5
Vomiting	-	1
Headache	17	9
Dizziness	4	2
Sleeplessness	5	6
Redness of skin	1	1
Blocked Nose	12	5
Eye Problem	10	3
Cough	3	-
Allergies	10	2
Wheezing	1	1

According to Trickler et al. (2010), silver nanoparticles may interact with cerebral micro vasculature and produce a pro inflammatory cascade which may further induce brain inflammation and neurotoxicity. Gliga et al. (2014) reported that silver nano particles (10 nm) were cytotoxic to human lung cells and the toxicity observed was associated with the level of intracellular silver (Ag) released in the cells. There was no past history of chronic or acute ill health among workers in jewellery units.

Anthropometric Measurements of Jewellery Unit Workers

Jewellery unit workers and the control group men did not show any significant differences in height and weight (p>0.05) of the study. Sungetal. (2009) reported that the sub chronic inhalation toxicity of silver nano particles was studied in Sprague- Dawley rats which indicated that there were no significant dose related differences in their body weight of exposed groups.

Table 6 shows the anthropometric measurements of workers employed in jewellery units

Table 6
Anthropometric Measurements of the Selected Jewellery Unit Workers

Anthro pometrics	Control group (A) (n=45)	Exposed groups Group (B) (n=148)	p Value (p<0.05)
Height (cm)$	156 (154-160)	154 (153-160)	0.228¥
Weight (Kg) *	68.42±9.70	62±10.70	0.115 †
BMI (Kg/m²)$	26.64 (23.9 - 30.4)	24.7 (22.9 - 27.9)	0.075¥
Systolic pressure$	119 (120-113)	123 (115 - 130)	0.223¥
Diastolic pressure*	75.05±7.75	78.20 ± 8.17	0.350†

$Median value (Inter quartile range)
*** Mean value ± standard deviation**
¥ Mann Witney test computed between the groups
Ŧ Student t test was computed

In the present study, there was no significant difference in body mass index (BMI) between exposed and control group workers ($p > 0.05$).

According to Kim et al. (2008) the oral toxicity of silver nano particles was studied in male and female Sprague-Dawley rats in which the rats did not show any significant changes in their body weight.

There was no significant difference in systolic blood pressure ($p>0.05$) of jewellery unit workers compared to the control (group A).

There was no significant difference ($p>0.05$) in diastolic blood pressure between the exposed group workers and control group.

Levels of Silver in Serum Among the Silver Jewellery Unit Workers

Workers of silver jewellery units had been exposed to hazardous compounds while processing. Silver is considered as xenobiotic compound with less known trace metal value in the human body. Therefore, the study was aimed to concentrate on silver jewellery workers who have been exposed to this metal daily over an extended period of time.

Several case studies of silver exposure showed that small doses of silver compounds taken as medication over several months might cause argyria in some humans. People who are working in silver compounds manufacturing factories inhale these compounds that may cause argyria. It may be due to thee levated level of silver in the air or duration of exposure at work place. It is also not known, what level of silver causes breathing problems, lung and throat irritation, or stomach pain in people (Agency for Toxic Substances and Disease Registry, 1990).

The level of silver in whole blood, plasma, serum or urine can be measured to know the health status and monitor the safety of exposed workers (Baselt, 2008). In the present study, level of serum silver was estimated in the jewellery unit workers.

The present study shows that serum silver level was significantly raised ($p<0.05$) in exposed groups (32μg/L) than control group (A). Raised level of silver in serum of jewellery unit workers could be due to exposure to fumes and dusts of silver emitted during the manufacturing process of silver jewellery.

Armitage et al. (1996) studied the uptake of silver in the blood of workers occupationally exposed to silver that showed the blood silver level ranging from 0.1 to 23.0 μg/L in which highest level of silver in blood was observed in reclaimers.

According to Eisses and Kaplan (2005), copper trafficking protein (ctr-1) can effectively transport silver into the cells exposed to even low micro molar concentration. 110AgNO3 injected rats showed that silver metabolism resembles that of copper with respect to tissue distribution. Silver does not significantly in hibit internal copper absorption but it affects copper metabolism as reported by Hansonetal. (2001). Estimation of silver level in the biological samples may help to characterize the individual degree of exposure and the occurrence of adverse consequences.

Similar to the present study, several researchers reported that increased level of silver in blood, serum and plasma of workers might be due to the occupational exposure of silver. Industrial workers are exposed to silver compounds from occupational settings namely jewellery and silver reclamation (Armitage et al., 1996), silver refineries and soluble and insoluble silver plant (Wolbling et al.,1988).

Hematological Indices in Jewellery Unit Workers

Red Blood Cell Indices

Table 7 presents the levels of red blood cell indices among workers employed in jewellery units

Table 7
Levels of Red Blood Cell Indices Among Jewellery Unit Workers

Red Blood Cell Indices	Control group (A) (n=45)	Exposed groups (n=148)	p Value
RBC$ (10^6 / µl)	4.97 (4.7- 5.29)	4.6 (4.28-4.94)	0.000¤
Hb* (g/ dl)	14.58 ± 1.2	13.54 ± 1.38	0.000¤
HCT* (%)	44.53± 3.48	40.61 ± 3.90	0.000¤
MCH$ (pg)	28.9 (27.75- 30)	29.7 (28.4 - 31.3)	0.003¤
MCHC$ (g/ dl)	32.6 (31.7- 3.2)	35.0 (32.3 - 36)	0.000¤
RDW$ (fl)	44.2 (41.8- 6.2)	45 (43.4 - 47)	0.177
MCV$ (fl)	88.6 (85.9- 1.5)	87.7 (82 - 93.7)	0.195

$ Median value (Inter quartile range)
Mann Witney test computed between the groups
*** Mean value ±standard deviation Student t test computed**
¤Statistically significant ($p<0.05$) compared to controls

Hematological indices were listed in Tables 7. The hematological profile such as RBC, HCT, and Hb levels of exposure group were found to be significantly decreased ($p<0.05$) compared to control group (A). Similarly, HCT level was significantly decreased in exposed group ($p<0.03$) than the control. MCH levels were increased significantly ($p<0.005$) in exposed group than the control group (A). In the exposed groups, MCHC level was significantly increased ($p<0.03$) in exposed group than control. Moreover, there was no significant difference between control and exposed groups of RDW (Table 7). An increase in MCH and MCHC in the present study might be due to exposure to pollutants in the jewellery units.

A similar result has been reported by Cheraghietal.(2014) in which RBC and hemoglobin levels were decreased considerably in male and female mice of silver nano particle treated groups than control group.

According to Shaluei et al. (2013), RBC count, Hb and HCT levels were significantly reduced in silver nanoparticle treated silver carp than control group.

The results of the present study are supported by the reduction in Hb level observed in oil refinery workers (Yartireh and Hashemian, 2013).

Mean corpuscular volume (MCV) and red blood cell distribution width (RDW) did not show any significant difference ($p>0.05$) between jewellery unit workers and control group of the study. Lee et al. (2013) reported that the hematological parameters such as MCV and RDW did not show significant changes after 28 daysof silver nanoparticle administration to Sprague Dawleyrats.

Total, differential leucocyte and platelet count

Table8 illustrates the total, differential leucocyte and plate let count in the blood of workers employed in the jewellery units.

White blood cells (WBC) or leucocytes are a part of the immune system. The type of leucocytes normally found in blood are lymphocytes, granulocytes (neutrophils, eosinophils and basophils) and monocytes (Chanetal.,2010). Therefore in the present study, measurement of blood leucocytes in the jewellery unit workers was found to be imperative to assess the influence of silver on immunological responses.

Total leukocyte count was observed significantly raising in number ($p<0.03$) in exposed group in contrast to control group (A). In differential counts such as lymphocytes and mixed cells (including basophils, eosinophils, and monocytes) counts were significantly increased ($p<0.001$) in exposed groups than the control group.

The number of mixed cells was significantly increased ($p<0.03$) in contrast with Control group. According to Sharma and Langer, (2014), an increase in number of differential leucocyte count (monocytes and eosinophils) was observed in fish (Garra gotyla gotyla) for 9 weeks of experimental duration by the effect ofmanganese.

The number of neutrophils did not show any significant difference between the control and exposed groups. Similar result was observed by Kianoush et al. (2013) in lead exposed workers.

Table 8
Total, Differential Leucocyte and Platelet Count in Blood among Jewellery Unit Workers

Hematological Indices	Control group (A) (n=45)	Exposed Group (B) (n=148)	pValue
WBC$ (10^3 /µl)	6.9 (5.8 - 7.6)	7.8 (6.5 - 8.5)	0.021
Lymphocytes$ (10^3 /µl)	2.6 (2.2 - 2.95)	3.0 (2.5 - 4.1)	0.000
Mixed cells$ (10^3 /µl)	0.8 (0.6 - 1.0)	1.0 (0.8 - 1.2)	0.000
Neutrophils$ (10^3 /µl)	3.6 (3.1 - 4.2)	3.3 (2.8 - 4.0)	0.323
Platelet* (10^3 /µl)	231.6 ± 51.5	246.4 ± 53.8	0.005
PDW$ (fl)	11.5 (10.7 - 12.3)	10.4 (9.2 - 12)	0.000
MPV$ (fl)	9.5 (9.0 - 9.8)	9.1 (8.1-10.1)	0.001

$ Median value (Inter quartile range)
Mann Witney test computed between the groups
*** Mean value ± standard deviation**
Student t test was computed with unequal sized samples
Statistically significant (p<0.05) compared to control

Platelet indices are potentially useful markers for the early diagnosis of thromboembolic diseases. An increase in both mean platelet volume (MPV) and platelet distribution width (PDW) due to platelet activation, resulting from platelet swelling and pseudopodia formation were hypothesized (Vagdatli et al., 2010).

From the study, though MPV and PDW were significantly decreased in exposed groups than control group, since the plate let count is normal, a low MPV and PDW do not mean much, because the size of the normal mature platelet issmall.

The results of the present study revealed some of the hematological values to be associated with silver absorption which is supported by the findings of Vlachou et al. (2007).

Pulmonary Function

Table 9

Pulmonary Function Parameters of Silver jewellery workers

Hematological Indices	Control group (A) (n=45)	Exposed Group (B) (n=148)	pValue
WBC$ (10^3 /µl)	6.9 (5.8 - 7.6)	7.8 (6.5 - 8.5)	0.021
Lymphocytes$ (10^3 /µl)	2.6 (2.2 - 2.95)	3.0 (2.5 - 4.1)	0.000
Mixed cells$ (10^3 /µl)	0.8 (0.6 - 1.0)	1.0 (0.8 - 1.2)	0.000
Neutrophils$ (10^3 /µl)	3.6 (3.1 - 4.2)	3.3 (2.8 - 4.0)	0.323
Platelet* (10^3 /µl)	231.6 ± 51.5	246.4 ± 53.8	0.005
PDW$ (fl)	11.5 (10.7 - 12.3)	10.4 (9.2 - 12)	0.000
MPV$ (fl)	9.5 (9.0 - 9.8)	9.1 (8.1 - 10.1)	0.001

Mean value ± standard deviation

Student t was computed for groups with unequal sized samples Statistically significant (p<0.05) compared to control

According to Bellamy (2011), the standard manoeuvre to assess lung function is a maximal forced exhalation with greatest effort possible after a maximum deep inspiration to total lung capacity. Several indices are derived from this manoeuvre. Lung function values are measured in litres and also expressed as a percentage of the predicted values for that individual. Predicted values are calculated from normal individuals. They vary with gender, height, age and ethnicity.

Forced vital capacity is the total volume of air expelled by a forced expiration after maximal inspiration (Matarese, et al., 2019). The Vital Capacity measures the vital capacity during low and deep inhalation. In patients with air flow limitation, VC is more accurate than the FVC. FVC value in comparison with predicted values is the most commonly examined parameter in routine spirometry testing as an indicator of restrictive process (Shapira et al.,2019).

FEV1 is the gold standard in clinical research to diagnose chronic obstructive pulmonary disease (COPD) and asthma (Chen et al., 2018). FEV1 and percentage predicted FEV1 values were not significantly different between the two groups. A study by Nakadate et al. (2006) among workers in toner manufacturing units also showed similar results.

FEV1/FVC and percentage predicted FEV1/FVC values were comparable between the two groups. Nwaghaetal. (2014) also found no differences in FEV1/FVC of cyclists exposed to traffic released carbon black. However, Neghab et al. (2019) reported a significantly decreased FEV1/FVC values in workers exposed to carbon black compared toreferents.

Maximum Mid Expiratory Flow and Peak Expiratory Flow

Percentage predicted FEF25-75, Peak Expiratory Flow and percentage predicted PEF of the participants are presented in Table 9. FEF25-75 measures the mean expiratory flow between 25 % and 75 % of the FVC, i.e., the mid volume of the expiratory flow (Hansen, 2011). It is a valuable measure in determining small airways function. Peak Expiratory Flow (PEF) is the maximal flow speed that can beachieved during a maximally forced expiration initiated at full inspiration (HarpreetRanu, 2011). Serial PEF monitoring is a useful confirmatory test for occupational as thmadiagnosis.

No significant difference was observed in percentage predicted FEF25-75 values between the two groups. Barrazza-Villarreal et al. (2011) found a significantly decreased FEF25-75 among children exposed to elemental carbon. However, the results of the present study are contradictory to their results.

PEF and percentage predicted PEF were not significantly lower among workers in the jewellery units. On the other hand, Albin et al. (1998) also reported asignificant decrease in PEF for subjects exposed to diesel exhaust when compared to those exposed to cleanair.

Maximum Ventilatory Volume is the volume of air exhaled in a specific period during rapid, forced breathing. MVV reflects muscle strength, airway resistance and compliance (Matarese et al., 2019). Percentage predicted MVV were not significantly different between the two groups.

Fig:3 Correlation Between Levels of Year of Exposure and FEV1/FVC Among Jewellery Unit Workers

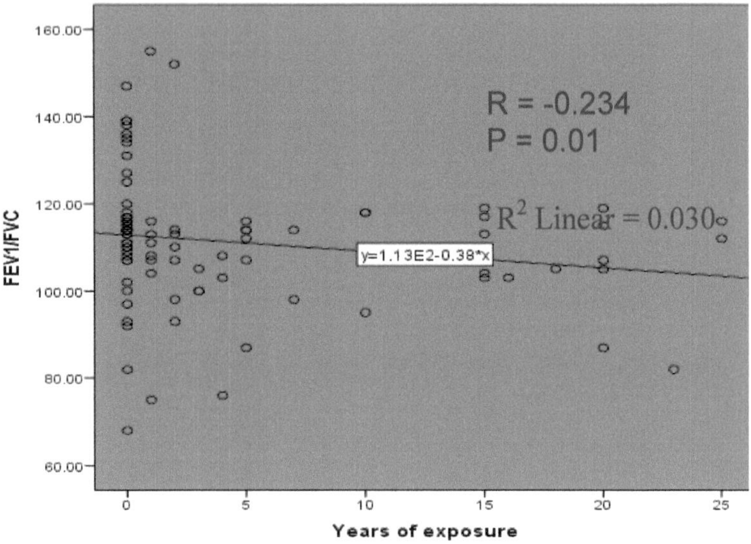

Year of exposure to airborne particles of silver jewellery unit was negatively correlated with the level of with FEV1/FVC ratio. (P = 0.01 and r = -0.234). However, no significant relationship was found between the year of exposure and other lung function parameters namely FVC, FIVC and FEF25-75.

A cause and effect relationship could not be established from cross-sectional studies, as in the present study. However, the significant negative correlation between the primary lung function outcome (FEV1/FVC) and year of exposure to airborne particles advocates a cause and effect relationship between the two.

Fig:4 Correlation Between Levels of Year of Exposure And FEV1 Among Jewellery Unit Workers

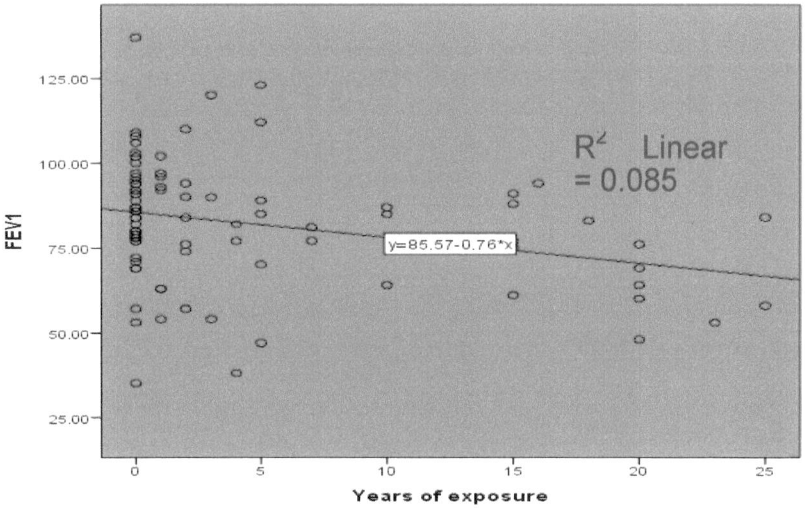

Year of exposure to dust and metal particles was negatively correlated with the level of with FEV1 (P = 0.005 and r =-0.291).

Barnes et al. (2009) stated that decline in FEV1 is an established marker for COPD. According to Barnesetal. (2009), MVV will be reduced in people with air flow obstruction, respiratory muscle weakness, poor coordination and poor effort. FEV1 (p=0.005) was found to be significantly inversely associated with the combined exposure to airborne particles of jewellery units, suggesting that combined exposure to jewellery unit particles and cigarette smoke might lead to obstructive lung diseases.

Fig:5 Correlation Between Levels of Year of Exposure And FVC Among Jewellery Unit Workers

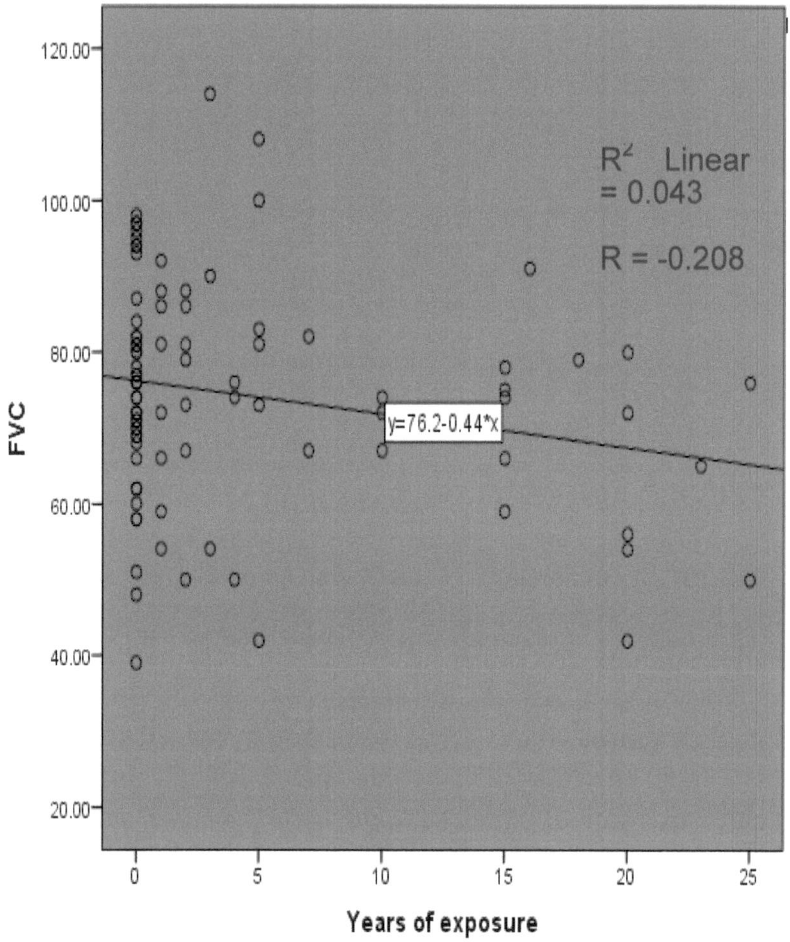

Year of exposure to jewellery unit was negatively correlated with the level of with FVC (P = 0.049 and r = -0.208).

Fig:6 Correlation Between Levels of Year of Exposure And PEFR Among In Jewellery Units

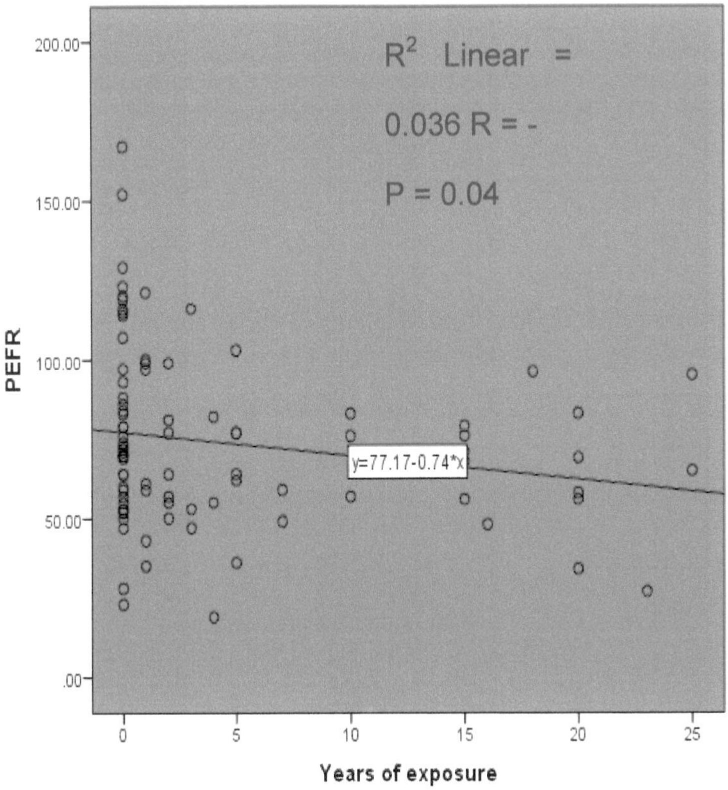

Year of exposure to jewellery units was negatively correlated with the level of with PEFR (P = 0.04 and r = - 0.204).

Fig:7 Correlation Between Levels of Year of Exposure and Lung Age Among Workers in Jewellery Units

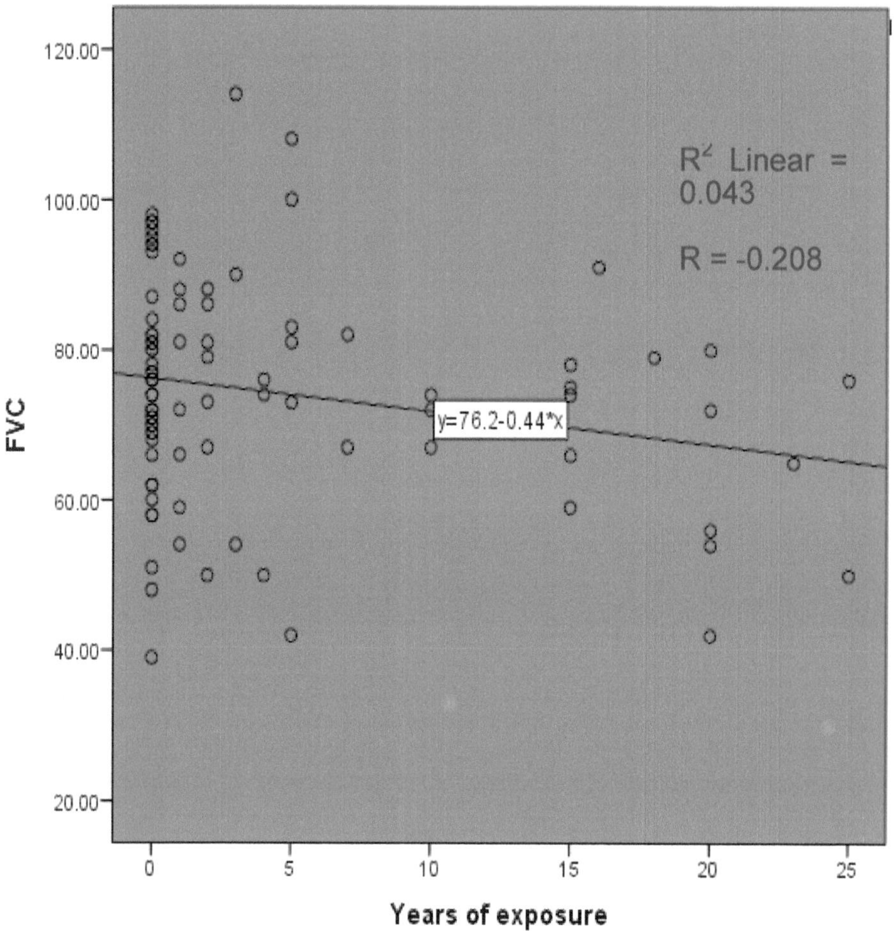

Year of exposure to air borne particles of jewellery unit was positively correlated with the lung age. (P = 0.08 and r =0.280).

Table 10
Correlation of Year of Exposure to Airborne Particles With Symptoms

Variables	Year of Exposure	Smoking habits	Throat Pain	Dry Skin	Decreased Appetite	Vomiting
Year of Exposure	1	0.032	-0.056	-0.280**	0.067	0.032
Smoking habits	-	1	0.034	0.145	-0.051	-0.058
Throat Pain	-	-	1	-0.085	-0.023	-0.024
Dry Skin	-	-	-	1		
Decreased Appetite	-	-	-	-	1	-0.011
Vomiting	-	-	-	-	-	1

**** = significance set at p<0.01 Pearson correlation was performed**

Year of exposure to airborne particle of jewellery unit was relatively correlated with the symptoms (Throat pain) of exposed workers. There was no significant difference between the smoking habits of exposed workers with symptoms.

Year of exposure to airborne particles of jewellery units was significantly inversely correlated with percentage predicted FEV1/FVC (R = -0.234 P = 0.01). Hnizdo et al 2002., implicated ther eduction in FEV1/FVC to obstructive lung diseases. Thus, in the present study, the negative relationship between the two suggests that exposure to jewellery workers to obstructive lung diseases. Similar to the results of the present study, Neghab et al. (2008) also reported an inverse relationship between exposure to carbon black and FEV1/FVC.

A cause and effect relationship could not be established from cross-sectional studies, as in the present study. However, the significant negative correlation between the primary lung function outcome (FEV1/FVC) and year of exposure advocates a cause and effect relationship between the two.

Correlation Between Year of Exposure to Jewellery Units and Pulmonary Function

Table 11 shows the correlation between year of exposure to jewellery units and pulmonary function. Spearman's correlation coefficient, rs, is a non parametric statistic and is used when the data is not normally distributed (Bernstein 2012).

Table11
Correlation Between Year of Exposure to Jewellery Units and pulmonary Function
(n = 47)

Lung function Parameters	Year of exposure	
	rs	p value
VC	0.059	0.539
F1VC	-0.028	0.775
PEF	-0.135	0.163
PIF	0.020	0.835
MVV	-0.075	0.440

rs - Spearman's rank correlation

According to Kurmi et al. (2013), a positive interaction indicates the combined effect of exposures is larger than the sum of the individual effects and a negative inter action represents a smaller combined effect than the sum of the individual effects. There were no significant difference in the pulmonary function parameters of exposed group and control group.

No significant correlation was observed between few lung function parameters (MVV, PIF, PEF, F1VC and VC) out come and year of exposure jewellery units between two groups of the study.

Biochemical markers

Glucose, protein, albumin and globulin

Levels of serum glucose, total protein, albumin in the participants are shown in Table12.

Table 12

Levels of Glucose, Total Protein, Albumin And Globulin

Biochemical marker	Control (n=45)	Jewellery unit workers (n=47)	p value
Glucose (mg/dl)	83.5 (76.5 - 103.6)	84.3 (78.4 - 109.4)	0.718
Protein (g/l)	72.8 (65.1 - 73.4)	74.5 (68.0 - 78.4)	0.242
Albumin (g/l)	39.3 (35.0 - 42.3)	35.3 (32.4 - 41)	0.015

Values are expressed as median (inter quartile range); p values for Mann Whitney test

Plasma glucose and total protein levels of jewellery unit workers were on par with those of the control subjects. However, serum album in levels, although with in the normal range, were significantly lower among the jewellery unit workers when compared to controls.

Don and Kaysen (2004) stated that serum albumin levels are decreased by systemic inflammation, acute liver disease, nephritic syndrome, malnutrition and protein losing enteropathies, whereas globulin levels are increased in liver diseases. It is a negative acute phase protein and its concentration is a marker of inflammation. Don and Kaysen (2004) stated that when album in concentration is reduced, other risk factors associated with both inflammation and cardiovascular risk are increased. In the present study, significantly decreased albumin level among jewellery units might be caused by inflammation occurring due to chronic exposure to pollutants from work place.

Enzymatic and Non Enzymatic Antioxidants

The major cellular antioxidants are enzymatic substances such as superoxide dismutase (SOD), glutathione peroxidase (GPx), catalase (CAT), Lipid peroxidation and various non-enzymatic low molecular substances such as vitamin E, vitamin A and vitamin C which act as various scavengers for different types of reactive oxygen species.

Table 13
Levels of Enzymatic And Non Enzymatic Antioxidant of Silver Jewellery Workers

Oxidative parameters	Control (n=45)	Exposed group (n=47)	p Value
Superoxide dismutase (SOD)	4.25±1.02	2.75±0.40	0.001
Catalase	0.86±2.8	1.45±2.45	0.085
Lipid Peroxidation	2.24±0.46	3.67±1.61	0.045
Glutathione peroxidase (GPX)	63.29±10.53	26.23±11.9	0.001
Glutathione S Transferase	6.44±0.64	5.18±0.32	0.123
Vitamin A	1.07±0.15	1.18±0.66	0.885
Vitamin C	82.77±12.03	83.61±11.61	0.564
Vitamin E	11.07±1.86	12.69±1.13	0.749

Mean value ± standard deviation
Student t test computed for groups with unequal sized samples Statistically significant ($p<0.05$) compared to control

Glutathione peroxidase (GPX) and Superoxide dismutase (SOD) were significantly decreased in exposed group than the control group. The other parameters did not show any significant difference among the two groups. The levels of Leukotriene B4 (LTB4) was negatively correlated with Glutathione peroxidase (GPX) ($r = -3.234$, $p = 0.002$) and Superoxide dismutase (SOD) ($r = -2.114$, $p = 0.001$). This indicates that lung inflammation occurs due to the exposure of airborne particle in work place environment.

Inflammatory Biomarkers

The role of biomarkers in assessing the adverse health effects of exposure is to link particle exposure to the clinical disease outcomes. Biomarkers are the detectable characteristic changes that reflect exposure-associated early events usually at biochemical and molecular levels.

Biomarker studies may provide mechanistic explanation to the adverse health effects. Increased levels of proinflammatory cytokines, cytokine receptors and C-reactive protein have been considered the biomarkers associated with air pollution induced systemic inflammation, platelet activation and increased expression of adhesion molecules have been identified as the biomarkers for the adverse cardiovascular effects of air pollution.

Plasma Clara cell protein and Leukotriene B4 levels

Table 14
Plasma Clara cell protein and Leukotriene B4

Inflammatory marker	Control (n = 45)	Jewellery units (n = 47)	p value
CC16 (ng/ml)	9.3 (3.45 - 22.7)	7.45 (4.32 - 23.12)	0.343
LTB4 (pg/ml)	12.8 (9.4 - 57.43)	74.63 (42.3 - 137.6)	<0.001

Values are expressed as median (inter quartile range); p values for Mann Whitney test

Levels of plasma Clara cell protein and leukotriene B4are presented in Table 14. CC-16 acts as an immunosuppressant and provides protection against oxidative stress and carcinogenesis. Serum levels rise following acute exposure to ozone, smoke, chlorine and lipopolysaccharide. The serum level of CC-16 is low in subjects with obliterative bronchiolitis, asthma and in smokers (Broeckaert and Bernard2000).

Leukotriene B4 (LTB4) is one of the most potent chemoattractants. It plays a pivotal role in inflammatory processes and stimulates polymorphonuclear leukocytes. LTB4 also leads to increased adhesion, degranulation, superoxide formation and cytotoxicity of these cells. It is also able to induce neutrophil accumulation in vivo. Elevated levels of LTB4 can be detected in diverse inflammatory disorders and contribute to the initiation or perpetuation of these diseases (Sugiyama et al., 2001).

No significant differences were observed in the CC16 levels between the two groups. Zuurbier et al. (2011) observed no significant association between long term traffic air pollution exposure and plasma CC16 levels. According to Sugiyama et al. (2001), acute exposures to certain pulmonary irritants as well as localized pulmonary inflammations could cause transient increases in serum CC16 levels, but might not be associated with measurable pulmonary damage or impairment of pulmonary function.

Levels of leukotriene B4 were significantly higher in exposed group. Significant rise in leukotriene B4 levels of the exposed group in the present study is suggestive of lung inflammation, which spills over into the circulation. The main effect of the pro- inflammatory eicosanoid leukotriene B4 is related to the inflammatory response and it facilitates capillary extravasation of neutrophils. (Aiello, et al.,2002).

Levels of Interleukin 8 and Myeloperoxidase (MPO)

Plasma levels of interleukins 8 and MPO of the participants are presented in Table14. Inter leukins are a group of pro-inflammatory cytokines (signaling molecules) that are expressed by leukocytes. Their primary functions are to stimulate inflammatory cell chemotaxis and to induce the maturation and prolife ration of immune cells including neutrophils, macrophages, T-helpercells, B-cells and natural killer cells. Interleukin-8 is a pro inflammatory chemokine (Morrow,2007).

Table 15
Levels of Interleukin 8 And Myeloperoxidase (Mpo) in Exposed Groups

Inflammatory markers	Control (n = 45)	exposed groups (n = 47)	p value
MPO (ng/ml)	234 (201- 289)	276 (234 - 341)	0.655
IL 8 (pg/ml)	16.4 (12.6 - 18.4)	19.2 (17.46 - 23.8)	0.001

Values are expressed as median (inter quartile range); p values for Mann Whitney test

Myeloperoxidase (MPO) is an enzyme stored in azurophilic granules of polymorpho nuclear neutrophils and macrophages and released into extra cellular fluid during inflammatory processes. Several studies have shown its involvement in oxidative stress and inflammation (Zhang et al., 2001). Plasma myeloperoxidase levels are useful in predicting theris kofatherosclerosis and coronary artery diseases.

Interleukin 8 levels were significantly higher among exposed group when compared to controls. According to Zuurbier et al. (2011) high plasma IL-8 levels indicate systemic inflammation and have been associated with cigarette smoking and COPD. In the present study, high levels of IL-8 among jewellery workers indicate systemic inflammation caused by chronic exposure to pollutants emitted during manufacturing process of jewellery units by volatile organic compounds and ultra fine particles. Increased levels of plasma IL 8 have been associated lung inflammation in COPD and asthma by Wouters et al. (2009).

Table: 16
Correlation Between Plasma Inflammatory Markers and Year of Exposure to Airborne Particles

Inflammatory markers	Year of Exposure	
	rs	p value
LTB4	0.212	0.001
CC16	-0.245	0.129
IL-8	0.264	0.003
MPO	0.013	0.859

rs= Sperman rank correlation on performed

Significant correlations between the inflammatory and antioxidant parameters were obtained by Spearman's correlation coefficient. Significant Negative correlation betweenSODandIL-6wasfoundintheexposedgroup(r=-0.612,p=0.05)compare to the control.

PHASE II

Genotoxicity Study

Exposure to genotoxic agents in occupational settings is often associated with an elevated risk for DNA damage. Most exposures in an occupational setting are chronic or repeated and the induced DNA damage might be expected to be elevated above baseline levels (Garaj-Vrhovac and Kopjar, 2009).

The comet assay or single cell gel electrophoresis is a simple and responsive method for studying DNA damage, and a useful tool for detection of genetic damage at the individual cell level (Tice et al., 2000). Based on the pulmonary function and oxidative status of workers, a sub population were selected for comet assay.

In the present study, based on the comet assay, no DNA damage wasobserved in exposed workers when compared to control. Mean tail moment (TM) value of the damage for control population was 1.23±0.16 while, for exposedworkers 1.37±0.84.

According to the observation of the present study, there was no significant difference in the intensity of DNA damage between control and exposed workers by comet assay.

PHASE III

Ambient Air Quality in Jewellery Units

Ambient air quality was assessed in a representative sample of three jewellery units. The results are presented in Table 17.

Table 17
Ambient Air Quality Jewellery Units of Coimbatore

Air quality parameter	Mean levels (n = 3)	Reference levels (NAAQS,2009)
Carbon monoxide (CO) (mg/m³)	<1.0	2.0
Fine particulate matter ($PM_{2.5}$) (µg/m³)	121 ± 44.2	60
Nitrogen di oxide (NO_2) (µg/m³)	5.4 ± 3.2	80
Ozone (O_3) (µg/m³)	<7.9	100
Particulate matter (PM_{10}) (µg/m³)	393.1 ± 33.5	100
Sulphur dioxide (SO2) (µg/m³)	2.7 ± 3.2	80

National Ambient Air Quality Standards, 2009

Ambient air quality in jewellery units shows the presence of high levels of particulate matter in these units. Similar results have been obtained by many investigators over the past decade (Nakadateetal.,1998; Tangetal., 2012 and Bello et al., 2012). The levels of other air quality parameters were within permissible limits in all the units.

SUMMARY OF THE STUDY 4

In the present study, silver jewellery unit workers were invited to participate in the program by individual approach and through prior participants. Free examinations, including blood tests and pulmonary function tests (PFT), were proposed to volunteer participants with occupational exposure to alloys and silver particles from the working environment.

Decrease in RBC indices and increased differential count, MCH, MCHC, PLT, PDW, and MPV levels might be due to exposure to Ag in the jewellery units. From the study results, it is evident that variations are observed and these variations though appear to be minimal are still deleterious.

No difference was observed in the prevalence of respiratory problems (mild, moderate or severe restriction and/or obstruction) between the exposed and unexposed participants of the study.

No differences were observed in the lung function between the exposed and unexposed groups. Year of exposure to airborne particles of jewellery units was inversely correlated with % predicted FEV1/FVC ($P = 0.01$ and $r = -0.234$).

Serum glucose and total protein levels of the jewellery workers were not significantly different when compare to control group. However, serum album in levels, although within the normal range, were significantly lower among the jewellery workers when compared to controls.

No significant difference was observed in the inflammatory markers such as clara cell protein and myeloperoxidase of exposed group when compare to control group. But levels of Interleukin 8 (IL-8), Leukotriene B4

(LTB4) were significantly increased in silver jewellery unit workers.

Year of exposure to air borne particles of jewellery units was positively correlated with levels of LTB4 (r=0.212, p=0.001) and Interleukin 8 (IL-8) (r=0.264, p=0.003). Significant rise in leukotriene B4 levels of the jewellery workers in the present study is suggestive of lung inflammation.

Glutathioneperoxidase (GPX) and Superoxidedismutase (SOD) were significantly decreased in exposed group than the control group. The levels of Leukotriene B4 (LTB4) was negatively correlated with Glutathione peroxidase (GPX) and Superoxide dismutase (SOD). This indicates that lung inflammation occurs due to the exposure of airborne particle in work place environment.

Based on the comet assay, no DNA damage was observed in exposed workers when compared to control. Mean tail moment (TM) value of the damage for control population was 1.23±0.16 while, for exposed workers 1.37±0.84. According to the observation of the present study, there was no significant difference in the intensity of DNA damage between control and exposed workers by comet assay.

Ambient air quality in jewellery units shows the presence of high levels of particulate matter in the work place whereas the levels of other air quality parameters were within permissible limits in all the units.

The findings of the study suggested that airborne particles of silver jewellery units caused transient moderate acute inflammation and oxidative stress might trigger the induction of inflammation.

BIBLIOGRAPHY

- Agency for Toxic Substances and Disease Registry - ATSDR. (1990), Toxicological Profile for Silver, Department of Health and Human Services, Public Health Service, TP-90-24, Atlanta, Georgia, United States, 157.

- Aiello,R., et al (2002), Leukotriene B4 receptor antagonism reduces monocytic foam cells in mice, Arterioscler. Thromb. Vasc, 22, 443-449.

- AlbinM,EngholmG,HallinN,HagmarL.(1998),Impactofexp osuretoinsulationwoolonlung function and cough in Swedish construction workers, Occup EnvironMed.,55(10),661-7.

- Albino Barraza-Villarreal, Jordi Sunyer, Leticia Hernandez-Cadena, Maria Consuelo Escamilla-Nuñez, Juan Jose Sienra-Monge, Matiana Ramírez-Aguilar, Marlene Cortez-Lugo, Fernando Holguin, David Diaz Sánchez, Anna Carin Olin, and Isabelle Romieu, (2008), Air Pollution, Airway Inflammation, and Lung Function in a Cohort Study of Mexico City Schoolchildren, Environ Health Perspect, 116(6),832–838.

- Alok Dhawan, Mahima Bajpayee, Alok Kumar Pandey, Devendra Parmar, (2002), Protocolfor the single cell gel electrophoresis/comet assay for rapid genotoxicity assessment, Developmental Toxicology Division Industrial Toxicology Research Centre ,Lucknow, U.P., India.

- American Diabetes Association - ADA. (2008), Diagnosis and classification of diabetes mellitus, Diabetes Care, 31(1), s55 - s60.

- Armitage,S.A.,White,M.AandWilson,H.K.(1996),Thedeter minationofsilverinwholeblood and its application to biological monitoring of occupationally exposed groups, Annals of Occupational Hygiene, 40(3), 331-338.

- Arora, S, Jain, J, Rajwade, J.M, Paknikar, K.M. (2008), Cellular responses induced by silver nanoparticles: In vitro studies. Toxicol Lett,179(2),93-100.

- Barnes, P.J. (2009), COPD as a disease of accelerated lung aging, Chest. 2009 Jan;135(1):173-180

- Baselt, R. (2008), Disposition of Toxic Drugs and Chemicals in Man, 8th Edition, Biomedical Publications, Foster City, California, 1429 - 1431.

- Bayfield, R.F. and Cole, E.R. (1980) Colorimetric determination of Vitamin A with Trichloroacetic acid. In: McCormick DB and Wright LD (ed.) Methods in Enzymology, Part F, Vitamins and coenzymes. Academic Press, NY, 189-95.

- Bellamy, D, Hutchison, D.C.(1981), The effects of salbutamol aerosol on lung function in patients with pulmonary emphysema, Br J Dis Chest, 75(2),190-6.

- Bernstein W.K. (2012), Pulmonary function testing, Curr Opin Anaesthesiol. 25(1):11-6.

- Bhattacharyya, A, Chattopadhyay, R, Hall, E.H, Mebrahtu, S.T, Ernst, P.B, Crowe, S.E. (2010), Mechanism of hypoxia-inducible factor 1 alpha-mediated Mcl1 regulation in Helicobacter pylori-infected human gastric epithelium. Am J Physiol Gastrointest Liver Physiol, 299,G1177–G1186.

- Blesi, M., Wise, B and Arney C.K. (2011), Medical Assisting: Administrative and Clinical Competencies, 7thEdition, Cangage Brain User, CiftonPark, United States of America, 1200.

- Broeckaert F, Bernard A. (2000),Clara cell secretory protein (CC16): Characteristics and perspectives as lung peripheral biomarker. Clin Exp Allergy, 30, 469–475.

- Buttarello, Mand Plebani, M.(2008), Automated Blood Cell Counts: State of the Art, American Journal of Clinical Pathology, 130, 104 - 116.

- Castellano,J.J,Shafii,S.M,Ko,F,Donate,G,Wright,T.E,Mannari,R.J,(2007),Comparative evaluation of silver-containing antimicrobial dressings and drugs. Int Wound J, 4(2),114-22.

- Catignani, G.L., (1986), An HPLC method for the simultaneous determination of retinol and alpha-tocopherol in plasma or serum, Methods Enzymol.,123:215-9.

- Centers for Disease Control and Prevention - CDCP. (2007), State-specific prevalence of cigarette smoking among adults and quitting among persons aged 18-35 years-United States-2006, Morbidity and Mortality Weekly Report (MMWR-Centers for Disease Control and Prevention), 56(38), 993 -996.

- Chan, Y.K., Tsai, M.H., Huang, D. C., Zong-Han Zheng, Z.H and Hung, K.D. (2010), Leukocyte nucleus segmentation and nucleus lobe counting, BMC Bioinformatics, 11(55), 1 - 16.

- ChenG, JiangL, WangL, ZhangW, CastilloC, FangX.(.2018), The accuracy of a handheld "disposable pneumotachograph device" in the spirometric diagnosis of airway obstruction in a Chinese population. Int J Chron Obstruct PulmonDis,13,2351-2360.

- Chen, X, Schluesener, H.J.(2008), Nanosilver: Anano product in medical application. Toxicol Lett, 176(1),1-12.

- Cheraghi, J., Hosseini, E., Hoshmandfar, R and Sahraei, R. (2014), Hematologic parameters study of male and female rats administrated with different concentrations of silver nanoparticles, International Journal of Agriculture and Crop Science, 7(10), 700 - 707.

- Dayal, H.H., Khuder, S., Sharrar, R and Trieff, N. (1994), Passive smoking in obstructive respiratory disease in an industrialized urban population, Environmental Research, 65(2), 161 - 171.

- Devasagayam,T.P.A.,Boloor,K.KandRamasarma,T.(2003), Methodsforestimationoflipid peroxidation: An analysis of merits and demerits, Indian Journal of Biochemistry and Biophysics, 40(5), 300 -308.

- Devasagayam,T.P.A.,Tilac,J.C.,Boloor,K.K.,Ketaki,S.S.,Saro j,S.DandLele,R.D.(2004), Free radicals and antioxidants in human health: Current status and future prospects, Journal of Association of Physicians of India, 52, 794 -804.

- Devi. J.S, Bhimba, B.V, Ratnam K. (2012), In vitro anticancer activity of silver nanoparticles synthesized using the extract of Gelidiella sp. J Pharm Pharm Sci, 4(4),710-5.

- Don, B.R, Kaysen, G.(2004), Serum albumin: relationship to inflammation and nutrition, Semin Dial. 17(6):432-7.

- Drake, P.L, Hazelwood, K.J.(2005), Exposure-related health effects of silver and silver compounds: A review. Ann Occup Hyg,49(7),575-85.

- E. Rojas, J. C. Ryu, Y. F. (2000) , Sasaki: Single cell gel/ Comet Assay: Guidelines for in vitro and in vivo genetic toxicology testing. Environ. Mol. Mutagen. 35, 206-221.

- Eisses, J.F and Kaplan, J.H. (2005), The mechanism of copper uptake mediated by human CTR1: A mutational analysis, The Journal of Biological Chemistry, 280(44), 37159 - 37168.

- Flora, S.J.S., Mittal, M and Mehta, A. (2008), Heavy metal induced oxidative stress and its possible reversal by chelation therapy, Indian Journal of Medical Research, 128(4), 501-523.

- Garaj-Vrhovac, V and Kopjar, N. (2009), Assessment of DNA sensitivity in peripheral blood leukocytes after occupational exposure to microwave radiation: The alkaline comet assay and chromatid breakage assay, Cell Biology and Toxicology,25(1),33-43.

- Ghaffari, M.A and Motlagh, B. (2011), In vitro effect of lead, silver, tin, mercury, indium and bismuthon human sperm creatine kinase activity: A presumable mechanism for men in fertility, Iranian Biomedical Journal, 15 (1-2), 38 -43.

- Gliga, A.R., Skoglund, S., Wallinder, I.O., Fadeel, B and Karlsson, H.L. (2014), Size- dependent cytotoxicity of silver nano particles in human lung cells: The role of cellular uptake, agglomeration and Ag release, Particle and Fibre Toxicology, 11(11), 1 - 17.

- Gulbranson, S.H, Hud, J.A, Hansen, R.C. (2000), Argyria following the use of dietary supplements containing colloidal silver protein. Cutis, 66(5), 373-4.

- Gulbranson, S.H., Hud, J.A., Hansen, R.C. (2000), Argyria following the use of dietary supplements containing colloidal silver protein, Cutis, 66(5), 373 - 384.

❖ Habig, W.H., Pabst, M.J., Fleishner, G., Gatmaitan, Z., Arias, I.M., Jakoby, W.B. (1974)Proc. Natl. Acad. Sei. USA, 71:3879.

❖ Haddam, N, Samira, S, Dumont, X, Taleb, A, Haufroid, V, Lison, D, Bernard, A. (2009), Lung epithelium injury biomarkers in workers exposed to sulphur dioxide in a non-ferrous smelter Hanson, S.R., Donley, S.A and Linder, M.C. (2001), Transport of silver in virgin and lactating rats and relation to copper, Journal of Trace Elements in Medicine and Biology, 15(4), 243 - 253.

❖ Harpreet Ranu, Michael Wilde, and Brendan Madden (2011), Pulmonary Function Tests, Ulster Med J, 80(2), 84-90.

❖ Hnizdo E, Sullivan PA,Bang KM, Wagner G. (2002), Association between chronic obstructive pulmonary disease and employment by industry and occupation in the US population: a study of data from the third national health and nutrition examination survey.Am J Epidemiol, 156,738-46.

❖ Jensen, E.J., Rungby, J., Hansen, J. C., Schmidt, E., Pedersen, B and Dahl, R. (1988), Serum concentrations and accumulation of silver in skin during three months treatment with ananti-smoking chewing gum containing silver acetate, Human and Experimental Toxicology, 7(6), 535 -554.

❖ Kademani, D. (2007), Oral Cancer, Symposium on Solid Tumors, Mayo Clinic Proceedings, 82(7), 878 - 887.

❖ Kaewamatawong, T., Banlunara, W., Maneewattanapinyo, P., Thammachareon, C and Ekgasit, S. (2014), Acute and subacute pulmonary toxicity caused by a single intratracheal instillation of colloidal silver nanoparticles in mice: Pathobiological changes and metallothionein responses, Journal of Environmental PathologyToxicology and Oncology, 33(1), 59 - 68.

❖ Kianoush, S., Mood, M.B., Mousavi, S.R., Shakeri, M.T., Dadpour, B., Moradi, V and Sadeghi, M. (2013), Clinical, toxicological, biochemical and hematologic parameters in lead exposed workers of a car battery industry, Iranian Journal of Medical Science, 38(1), 30 - 37.

❖ Kim, Y.S, Kim, J.S, Cho, H.S, Rha, D.S, Kim, J.M, Park,J.D. (2008),Twentyeight-day oral toxicity, genotoxicity, and gender-related tissue distribution of silver nanoparticles in Sprague- Dawley rats. Inhal Toxicol,20(6):575-83.

❖ Kim, Y.S., Kim, J.S., Cho, H.S., Rha, D.S., Kim, J.M., Park, J.D., Choi, B.S., Lim, R., Chang, H.K., Chung, Y.H., Kwon, I.H., Jeong, J., Han, B.S and Yu, I.J. (2008), Twenty-eight-day oral toxicity,genotoxicity,andgender-related tissued is tribution of silver nano particles in Sprague - Dawley rats, Inhalation Toxicology, 20(6), 575 -583.

❖ Krott M.M.C., Münchow, M., Pirev, E., Hessner, F., Bozkurt, A., Uciechowski, P., Pallua, N., Kröncke, K.D and Suschek C.V. (2009) , Silver ions induce oxidative stress and intracellular zinc release in human skin fibroblasts, Free Radical Biology and Medicine, 47(11), 1570 - 1577.

- Kurmi,O.P, Devereux, G.S, Smith, W.C, Semple, S, Steiner, M.F, Simkhada, P, LamK.B, Ayres, J.G. (2013), Reduced lung function due to biomass smoke exposure in young adults in rural Nepal, Eur Respir J. 2013Jan;41(1):25-30.

- Lakind JS, Holgate ST, Ownby DR . A critical review of the use of Clara cell secretory protein (CC16) as a biomarker of acute or chronic pulmonary effects. Biomarkers. 2007;12:445–467. Lansdown, A.B.G. (2002), Silver I: Its antibacterial properties and mechanism of action, Journal of Wound Care, 11,125 - 138.

- Lansdown, A.B.G. (2010), A pharmacological and toxicological profile of silver as an antimicrobial agent in medical devices, Advanced Pharmacological Science, 2010, 16.

- Lee, J.H., Kim, Y.S., Song, K.S., Ryu, H.R., Sung, J.H., Park, J.D., Park, H.M., Song, N.W., Shin, B.S., Marshak, D., Ahn, K., Lee J.E and Yu, I.J. (2013), Biopersistence of silver nanoparticles in tissues from Sprague Dawley rats, Particle and Fibre Toxicology, 10(36), 1 - 14.

- Luck, 1974, In: Methods in enzymatic analysis, 2 nd Edition, New York: Bergmayer Academic press, 805.

- MatareseA, SarduC, ShuJ, SantulliG.(2019), Why is chronic obstructive pulmonary disease linked to a trial fibrillation: A systematic overview of the under lying mechanisms. Int. J.Cardiol, 276,149-151.

- Morrow,D.A.(2007),"Appraisalofmyeloperoxidaseforevaluationofpatientswithsuspected acute coronary syndromes," Journal of the American College of Cardiology, 49(20), 2001- 2002.

- Nakadate,Y.Aizawa,T.Yagami,Y.Q.Zheg,M.Kotani,andK.IshiwataT.(1998),Changein obstructive pulmonary function as a result of cumulative exposure to welding fumes as determinedbymagnetopneumographyinJapanesearcwelders,OccupEnvironMed,55(10): 673-677.

- National Institute for Occupational Safety and Health - NIOSH. (2003), Registry of Toxic Effects of Chemical Substances (RTECS): Silver, Cincinnati, Ohio, United States of America, 186.

- Neghab M, Ebrahimi A, Soleimani E,(2019), Respiratory symptoms and lung functional impairments associated with occupational exposure to poultry house pollutants, Int J OccupSaf Ergon. 11,1-7.

- Nij,E.T.,Hilhorst,S.,Spee,T.,Spierings,J.,Steffens,F.,Lumens, MandHeederik,D.(2003), Dust control measures in the construction industry, The Annals of Occupational Hygiene, 47 (3), 211 - 218.

- Nordberg, G. F., Fowler, B.A., Nordberg, M and Friberg, L. (2011), Handbook on the Toxicology of Metals, 4rd Edition, Academic Press, London, United Kingdom, 1, 1542.

- Nwagha U, Iyare E, Anyaehie U, Onyedum C, Okereke C, Ajuzieogu O, AmucheaziA, Oluboboku T, Agu P, Igweh J, Oguanuo T.(2014), Ann Med Health Sci Res. 2014 Jul;4(4):516-21.

- Olive P L and Bantah J P. (2006), The comet assay: a method to measure DNA damage in individual cells, Nat Protoc.1(1),23-9.

- Panyala,N.P,Mendze,E.M,Havel,J.(2008)Silverorsilvernano particles:Ahazardousthreat to the environment and human health?, J Appl Biomed,6(3),117-29.

- Panyala, N.P., Mendze, E.M.P and Havel, J. (2008), Silver or silver nanoparticles: A hazardous threat to the environment and human health?, Journal of Applied Biomedicine,6(3), 117 -129.

- Rehm, J., Baliunas, D., Borges, G.L.G., Graham, K., Irving, H., Kehoe, T., Parry, C.D., Patra, J., Popova, S., Poznyak, V., Roerecke, M., Room, R., Samokhvalov, A.V and Taylor, B. (2010), The relation between different dimensions of alcohol consumption and burden of disease: An overview, Addiction, 105 (5), 817 - 843.

- Repace, J. L. (1981), The problem of passive smoking, Bulletin of the New York Academy of Medicine, 57(10), 936 - 946.

- RotruckJ.T.,PopeA.L.,GantherH.E.,SwansonA.B.,Hafeman D.G.andHoekstraW.G. (1973), Selenium: biochemical role as a component of glutathione peroxidase. Science 179, 588-590.

- Sanchez-Huerta, V., De Wit-Carter, G., Hernandez-Quintela, E and Naranjo-Tackman, R. (2003), Occupational corneal argyrosis in art silver solderers, Cornea, 22(7), 604 - 611.

- Shaluei, F., Hedayati, A., Jahanbakhshi, A., Kolangi, H and Fotovat, M. (2013), Effect of subacute exposure to silver nanoparticle on some hematological and plasma biochemical indices in silver carp (Hypophthalmichthys molitrix), Human and experimental toxicology, 32(12), 1270 - 1277.

- Shapira U, Krubiner M, Ehrenwald M, Shapira I, Zeltser D, Berliner S, Rogowski O, Shenhar- Tsarfaty S, Bar-Shai A. (2019), Eosinophil levels predict lung function deterioration in apparently healthy individuals. Int J Chron Obstruct Pulmon Dis,14:597-603.

- Sharma,B.R.,Harish,D.,Singh,V.PandBangar,S.(2006),Septicemiaasacauseofdeath in burns: An autopsy study, Burns, 32(5), 545 -549.

- Sharma, M., Salisbury, R.L., Maurer, E.I., Hussain, S.M and Sulentic, C.E. (2013), Gold nanoparticles induce transcriptional activity of NF-κB in a B-lymphocyte cell line, Nanoscale, 5(9), 3747 - 3756.

- Singh, N., Kumar, D and Sahu, A.P. (2007), Arsenic in the environment: Effect on human health and possible prevention, Journal of Environmental Biology, 28, 259 - 365.

❖ Sivakuma,rP,Nethradevi,C,Renganathan,S.(2012),Synthesi sofsilvernanoparticlesusing Lantana camara fruit extract and its effect on pathogens. Asian JPharmClinRes, 5(3), 97-101.

❖ Stanley, T. Omaye , Ellen E. Schaus , Mark A. Kutnink , Wayne C.Hawkes, (1987) Measurement of Vitamin C in Blood Components by High-Performance Liquid Chromatograph Implication in Assessing Vitamin C Status, Annals of the New York Academy of Science.

❖ Sue, Y.M, Lee, J.Y, Wang, M.C, Lin, T.K, Sung, J.M, Huang, J.J. (2001),Generalized argyria in two chronic hemodialysis patients. Am J Kidney Dis, 37(5),1048-51.

❖ Sugiyama, S,Y. Okada, G. K. Sukhova, R. Virmani, J. W. Heinecke, and P. Libby, (, 2001) "Macrophage myeloperoxidase regulation by granulocyte macrophage colony-stimulating factor in human atherosclerosis and implications in acute coronary syndromes," American Journal of Pathology, 158(3),879–891.

❖ Sullivan, J.B and Krieger, G.R. (2001), Clinical Environmental Health and Toxic Exposures, 2ndEdition, Lippincott Williams and Wilkins Publishers, Philadelphia, United State of America, 1295.

❖ Sung,J.H.,Ji, J.H., Park, J.D., Yoon, J.U., Kim, D.S., Jeon, K.S., Song, M.Y., Jeong, J., Han, B.S., Han, J.H., Chung, Y.H., Chang, H.K and Lee, J.H.(2009), Subchronic inhalation toxicity of silver nanoparticles, Toxicological Sciences, 108(2), 452 –461.

- Suzuki Y.J., Packer L. Inhibition of NF-κB activation by vitamin E derivatives. Biochem. Biophys. Res. Commun. 1993; 193:277–283.

- Tice, R.R. Agurell, E D. Anderson, B. Burlinson, A. Hartmann, H. Kobayashi, Y. Miyamae, Trickler, W.J., Lantz, S.M., Murdock, R.C., Schrand, A.M., Robinson, B.L., Newport, G.D., Schlager, J.J., Oldenburg, S.J., Paule, M.G., Slikker, W., Hussain , S.M and Ali S.F. (2010), Silver nanoparticle induced blood-brain barrier inflammation and increased permeability in primary rat brain microvessel endothelial cells, Toxicological Science,118(1), 160 - 170.

- Vagdatli, E., Gounari, E., Lazaridou, E., Katsibourlia, E., Tsikopoulou, F and Labrianou, I. (2010), Platelet distribution width: A simple, practical and specific marker of activation of coagulation, Hippokratia, 14(1), 28 - 32.

- Vlachou, E., Chipp, E., Shale, E., Wilson, Y.T., Papini, R and Moiemen, N.S. (2007), The safety of nanocrystalline silver dressings on burns: A study of systemic silver absorption, Burns, 33(8), 979 - 985.

- Wan, A.T., Conyers, R.A.J., Coombs, C.J and Masterton, J.P. (1991), Determination of silver in blood, urine and tissues of volunteers and burn patients, Clinical Chemistry, 37, 1683 - 1687.

- Ward, P (2014), Testicular distribution and toxicity of a novel LTA4H inhibitor in rats, Toxicol. Appl. Pharmacol., 278, 26-30.

- Watanabe, J. (2004), Synthesis and structural characterization of silver(I), aluminium(III) and cobalt(II) complexes with 4-isopropyltropolone (hinokitiol) showing noteworthy biological activities. Action of silver(I)-oxygen bonding complexes on the antimicrobial activities. J Inorg Biochem, 98(1), 46-60.

- Weir, F.W. (1979), Health hazard from occupational exposure to metallic copper and silver dust, American Industrial Hygiene Association Journal, 40(3), 245 - 247.

- Wells, A.J.(1994), Passive smoking as a cause of heart disease, Journal of American College of Cardiology, 24(2), 546 -554.

- Wheeler, P. R and Gregory, D. (1980), Superoxide Dismutase, Peroxidatic Activity and Catalase in Mycobacterium Zeprae Purified from Armadillo Liver Journal of General Microbiology, 121, 457-464.

- Wolbling, R.H., Milbradt, R., Schopenhauergermann, E., Euler, G and Konig, K.H. (1988), Argyrosis in employees of the silver processing industry, Arbeitsmedizin Sozialmedizin Praventivmedizin, 23(12), 293 - 297.

- World Health Organization - WHO, (1999), Hazard prevention and control in the work environment: Airborne dust, Occupational health, Geneva, Switzerland, 246.

- World Health Organization - WHO, (2008), WHO Report on the Global Tobacco Epidemic2008: The MPOWER Package, Geneva, Switzerland, 342.

- Xia, T, Kovochich, M, Brant, J, Hotze, M, Sempf, J, Oberley, T. (2006), Comparison of the abilities of ambient and manufactured nanoparticles to induce cellular toxicity according to an oxidative stress paradigm. Nano Lett, 6(8),1794-807.

- Yartireh, H.A and Hashemian, A.H. (2013), The effect of occupational exposure to lead on blood hemoglobin concentration in workers of kermanshah oil refinery, Iranian Journal of Toxicology, 6(19), 766 - 770.

- Zhang R, Brennan M-L, Fu X, (2001), Association between myeloperoxidase levels and risk of coronary artery disease. Journal of the American Medical Association,286(17),2136–2142.

- Zhu, K., Moriarty, C., Caplan, L.S and Levine, R.S. (2007), Cigarette smoking and primary liver cancer: A population-based case-control study in USmen, Cancer Causes and Control, 18(3), 315 -321.

- Zuurbier M, Hoek G, Oldenwening M, Meliefste K, Krop E, van den Hazel P, BrunekreefB.(2011), In-traffic air pollution exposure and CC16, blood coagulation, and inflammation markers in healthy adults, Environ Health Perspect.,119(10),1384-9.

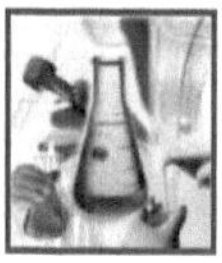

APPENDICES

Appendix - 1
Questionnaire Administered to the Workers of Jewellery Units

1. Name : Date:
2. Sex: Female/Male
3. Age:
4. Height:
5. Weight:
6. Office address:
7. Residential address:
8. Telephone:
9. Occupation:
10. Work experience: Income:
11. Please circle the highest year of school completed:
    1 2 34 5 6 7 8 9 10 11 12
    (Primary) (High School) (College/University)
12. Are you: Married/Single
13. Smoking habits:
14. No of cigarettes/day: Years:
15. Passive smoking: Ex smoker:
16. Do you have any other addictions?

Professional Background

17. Working hours/day:
18. No of working days/week:
19. What chemicals/alloys do you use in your working area?
20. Number of years in jewellery units:

Health Survey

21. In the past week did you ever have any of the following symptoms?

Throat pain?	☐No☐Yes...............Duration
Dry skin?........................	☐No☐Yes .... Duration
Decreased appetite?	☐No☐Yes..............Duration
Nausea or vomiting?...........	☐No☐Yes..............Duration
Abdominal pain?	☐No☐Yes ....Duration
Headaches?	☐No☐Yes..............Duration
Dizziness?	☐No☐Yes..............Duration
Sleeplessness?	☐No☐Yes..............Duration
Redness of skin?	☐No☐Yes..............Duration
Blocked nose, runny nose/sneezing fits...	☐No☐Yes..............Duration
Eye problems/ irritations? ...	☐No☐Yes..............Duration
Persistent cough?	☐No☐Yes..............Duration
Asthma?	☐No☐Yes..............Duration
Wheezing?	☐No☐Yes..............Duration
Allergies?	☐No☐Yes..............Duration
Muscle weakness?	☐No☐Yes..............Duration

Frequency of attacks : Seasonal / throughout the year

22. Do you have any other symptoms, which are not covered by this questionnaire?

Clinical History

23. Please indicate below which chronic condition(s) you have: (if any)
    Diabetes:
    High cholesterol:
    Liver diseases:
    Nervous tension:
    Skin diseases:
    Kidney stones:
    Kidney diseases:
    Jaundice:
    Other chronic condition specifies :
    Do you currently use any medication regularly?
    If yes how long have you been taking this medication?

Life Style

24. Diet:
    Do you include fresh fruits and vegetables in your diet?
    No ☐ Yes ☐
    Do you, in your leisure time, regularly play sports/do exercise?
    No ☐ Yes ☐
    Do you limit your intake of fats in your diet?
    No ☐ Yes ☐
    Do you drink alcohol?
    No ☐ Yes ☐
    How often and how much do you have?
    No ☐ Yes ☐

Awareness about Emissions from Jewellery Units

25. Do you know about emissions from the jewellery unit?
    No ☐ Yes ☐

26. What have you done/ intend to do about the emissions from the jewellery unit?

Informed Consent

Informed consent form for participants who are participating in the research on health status of workers in jewellery units

Principal Investigator : DrK.V.Shalini
Organisation : Rathnavel Subramaniam College of Arts and Science, Sulur, Coimbatore
Name of the proposal : An Observational Cross Sectional Study on Pulmonary Function, Oxidative Stress, Inflammatory Biomarkers and Genotoxicity among Workers in Silver Jewellery Units,Coimbatore

The informed consent form has two parts:

1. Information sheet (to share information about the research withyou)
2. Certification of consent (for signature if you agree to take part)

You will be given a copy of the full Informed consent form

Part II: Certificate of Consent

I have read the foregoing information, or it has been read to me. I have had the opportunity to ask questions about it and any questions that I have asked have been

answered to my satisfaction. I consent voluntarily to participate as a participant in this research.

Print the name of Participant --

Signature of Participant ---

Date --

If Illiterate

I have witnessed the accurate reading of the consent form to the potential participant, and the individual has the opportunity to ask questions. I confirm that the individual has given consent freely.

Print name of witness ----------- and Thumb print of participant

Signature of witness --------------

Date ---------------------------------

Statement by the Researcher/Person taking Consent

I have accurately read out the information sheet to the potential participant and to the best of my ability made sure that the participant understands that the following will be done:

1. Collection of blood sample (5ml)
2. Pulmonary Function AnalysisTest

I confirm that the participant was given an opportunity to ask questions about the study and all the questions asked by the participant have been answered correctly and to the best of my ability. I confirm that the individual has been coerced into giving consent and the consent has been given freely and voluntarily.

A copy of this ICF has been provided to the participant.

Print Name of Researcher/Person taking the Consent-----------------------

Signature of Researcher/Person taking the Consent -------------------------

Date----------------------------- -

Appendix - 2
Assessment of Haematological Indices in Blood Haematology Analyzer KX-21 (Sysmex Corporation, Kobe, Japan)

The KX-21 performs quick and accurate analysis of 18 parameters in blood and it contains three detector blocks for blood analysis. WBC count is measured by the WBC detector block using the DC detection method. The RBC count and platelets are taken by the RBC detector block using the DC detection method. The HGB detector block measures the haemoglobin concentration using the noncyanide hemoglobin method. HCT detector block measures the hematocrit value using the RBC pulse height detection methods.

Equipment : Sysmax KX-21 Analyzer
Manufacturer : Sysmex Corporation Type
Throughput : 60samples/hour
Haematology Analyzer Parameters : WBC, RBC, HGB, HCT, MCV, MCH, MCHC, PLT, NEUT%, LYMPH%, MXD%, NEUT#, LYMPH#, MXD#, RDW, PDW, MPV, and P-LCR.
Method: Electrical Impedance

Reagent
Cell pack (30 L) - Diluent

Analysis Parameters

This instrument analyzes the following parameters using three detector blocks with one reagent.

Parameters	Description
White Blood Cell (WBC)	Number of WBC in 1μL of whole blood
Lymphocyres % **(LYM%)**	Ratio (%) of lymphocytes (small cells) to whole WBC
Mixed cells % **(MXD%)**	Ratio (%) of the summation of basophils, eosinophils and monocytes (middle cells) to whole WBC
Neutrophils % **(NEUT%)**	Ratio (%) of neutrophils (large cells) to whole WBC
Lymphocyres # **(LYM#)**	Absolute count of lymphocytes (small cells) in1 μL of whole blood.
Mixed cells # **(MXD#)**	Absolute count of the summation of basophils, eosinophils and monocytes (middle cells) in1 μL of whole blood
Neutrophils # **(NEUT#)**	Absolute count of lymphocytes (large cells) in1 μL of whole blood
Red blood cells **(RBC)**	RBC count in1 μL of whole blood
Haemoglobin **(HGB)**	Volume (g) of haemoglobin in 1 dL of whole blood
Hematocrit value **(HCT)**	Ratio (%)of whole RBC volume in whole blood
Mean RBC volume **(MCV)**	Means RBC volume (fL) in whole blood which is calculated by Hct/RBC
Mean RBC haemoglobin **(MCH)**	Mean hemoglobin volume (pg) per RBC which is calculated by Hgb/RBC
Mean RBC haemoglobin concentration **(MCHC)**	Mean hemoglobin concentration (g/dL) which is calculated by Hgb/RBC
RBC distributed width **(RDW)**	The distributed width (fL) at the height of 20% from the bottom when the peak RBC particle distribution curve is taken as100%
Platelet **(PLT)**	Platelet count in 1 mL of whole blood
Platelet distributed width **(PDW)**	The distributed width (fL) at the height of 20% from the bottom with the peak of platelet particle curves taken as 100%
Mean platelet volume **(MPV)**	Mean volume of platelet (fL)

Procedure

Blood is well mixed and placed on a rack in the analyzer. This instrument has flow cells, photometers and apertures that analyze different elements in the blood. The cell counting component counts the numbers and types of different cells within the blood. The results are sent to a computer for review or printed out. Blood counting machines aspirate a very small amount of the specimen through narrow tubing followed by an aperture and a laser flow cell. Laser eye sensors count the number of cells passing through the aperture and can count them on flow cytometry method. The two main sensors used are light detectors and electrical impedance. The instrument measures the type of blood cell by analyzing data about the size and aspects of light as they pass through the cells (called front and side scatter). In addition to counting, it measures and analyzes red blood cells, white blood cells and platelets. It also measures the amount of hemoglobin in the blood and within each red blood cell. This is done by adding a diluent that lyses the cells which is then pumped into a spectrophotometric measuring cuvette. The change in color of the lysate equates to the hemoglobin content of the blood.

Appendix - 3
Estimation of Silver in Serum
(Flame Atomic Absorption Spectroscopy (FAAS) method - Wan et al., 1991)

Principle

Atomic absorption spectroscopy is a spectroanalytical process used to determine the quantity of chemical elements using the optical radiation absorption by free atoms within gaseous state. The technique follows the absorption spectrometry to know the concentration of an analyte within the sample, the electrons within the atoms put to higher orbitals for little time by making them absorb a great amount of energy.

Specifications

Equipment	:	SHIMADZU, AA-7000
Wave length range	:	185 – 900nm
Hollow-cathode lamp:		Six lamps, automatic setup
Accuracy management	:	QA/QC functions
Background correction method	:	D2 or SR methods selectable
Atomizer	:	Dual atomizer (automatic flame/furnace switching)
Photometric mode photometric system	:	Optical double-beam
Silver calibrator	:	1mg/L silver nitrate stock solution was prepared and that was serially diluted with double distilled water to give concentrations of 1, 5, 10, 50 and 100 µg/L silver nitrate.

Procedure

5ml of diluted serum sample was pre-treated with 0.5 ml of concentrated nitric acid. Evaporated the sample to near dryness on a hotplate and cooled. Then added 0.5 ml of nitric acid, the additional acid treatment was necessary to complete digestion. The pretreated sample was introduced into the flame atomic absorption spectroscopy (FAAS) at the wavelength of 328 nm with a slit width of 0.7 nm. The signal peak areas were automatically integrated over 5 s to calculate the results.

The sera samples was used to analyze the presence of Silver (Ag) levels in the exposed and control group workers. Working standards of CdCl2, ZnSO4, CuSO4 and AgNo3 was prepared by 1000 µg/ml, 1000 µg/ml, 1025 µg/ml and 100 µg/L, respectively. Cd, Zn and Cu were determined by graphite furnace AAS flame at 229, 213 and 325respectively).

Appendix - 4
Estimation of Glucose in Serum
(GOD-PAP method – Trinder, 1969)

Principle

Enzymatic determination of glucose based on following reaction:

$$\text{Glucose} + O_2 + H_2O \xrightarrow{\text{Glucose oxidase}} H_2O_2 + \text{Gluconicacid}$$

Per oxidase

$$2H_2O_2 + \text{Phenol} + 4 - \text{Aminophenazone} \longrightarrow \text{Quinonimine} + 4H_2O$$

Reagents

1. Glucose reagent : 92 mmol/L of Tris Buffer (pH 7.4), 0.3 mmol/L of Phenol,15000U/L of Glucose oxidase, 2.6 mmol/L of 4 -Aminophenazone
2. Glucose Standard (100mg/dl)

Procedure

Pipetted into tubes marked	Blank	Standard	Test
Reagent	1000μl	1000μl	1000μl
Standard	-	10μl	-
Serum	-	-	10μl

Mixed and incubated for 10 minutes at 37° C. Read the absorbance of standard and sample at 505 nm against the reagent blank.

Calculation

Calculated the results as follows

$$\text{Albumin(g/dl)} = \frac{\text{Absorbance of Test}}{\text{Absorbance of Standard}} \times \text{Concentration of Standard(mg/dl)}$$

Appendix - 5
Estimation of Albumin in Serum
(BCG Dye method, End point - Doumas, 1971)

Principle

Albumin binds with bromocresol green (BCG) at pH 4.2 causing a shift in absorbance of the yellow BCG dye. The blue - green colour formed is proportional to the concentration of albumin present, when measured photometrically between 580-630 nm with maximum absorbance at 625nm.

Reagents

Albumin reagent : 0.08 mmol/L of Bromocresol green, 50mmol/L of Succinate buffer (pH 4.2), 1 gm/L of Sodiumazide

Albumin Standard (3.6 mg/dl)

Procedure

Pipetted into tubes marked	Blank	Standard	Test
Albumin reagent	1000µl	1000µl	1000µl
Distilled water	10µl	-	-
Standard	-	10µl	-
Serum	-	-	10µl

Mixed well and read the absorbance of standard and samples at625nm (580- 630 nm) against reagent blank, after one minute incubation at37°C.

Calculation

Calculated the results as follows:

$$\text{Albumin(g/dl)} = \frac{\text{Absorbance of Test}}{\text{Absorbance of Standard}} \text{ X Concentration of Standard(mg/dl)}$$

Appendix - 6

Estimation of Total Protein in Serum (Biuret method, End point - Young et al., 1975)

Principle

The peptide bonds of protein react with copper II ions in alkaline solution to form blue violet complex (biuret reaction), each copper ion complexing with 5 or 6 peptide bonds. Tartarate is added as a stabilizer whilst iodide is used to prevent auto reduction of the alkaline copper complex. The colour formed is proportional to the protein concentration and is measured at 546 nm.

Reagents

Total protein reagent: 19 mmol/L of Copper ll sulphate, 43 mmol/L of Potassium sodium tartrate, 30 mmol/L of Potassium iodide, 600 mmol/L of Sodium hydroxide. Protein Standard (6.0g/dl)

Procedure

Pipetted into tubes marked	Blank	Standard	Test
Total protein reagent	1000µl	1000µl	1000µl
Distilled water	20µl	-	-
Standard	-	20µl	-
Serum	-	-	20µl
Incubated for 10 minutes at 37°C			

Measured the absorbance of the standard and samples at 546nm (520-560 nm) against reagent blank.

Calculation

Calculated the results as follows:

$$\text{Total protein(mg/dl)} = \frac{\text{Absorbance of Test}}{\text{Absorbance of Standard}} \times \text{Concentration of Standard (mg/dl)}$$

Appendix - 7

Estimation of Catalase activity
Spectrophotometry method (Luck, 1974)

Catalase has a double function as it catalyzes the following reactions:

a) Decomposition of hydrogen peroxide (H_2O_2) to give water and oxygen.

$$2H_2O_2 \xrightarrow{\text{Catalase}} 2H_2O + O_2$$

b) Oxidizes H+ donors, for example methanol, formic acid, phenol with the consumption of one mole of peroxide.

$$ROOH + AH_2 \xrightarrow{\text{Catalase}} H_2O + ROH + A$$

Principle

The UV light absorption of hydrogen peroxide solution can be easily measured between 230 and 250nm. On decomposition of hydrogen peroxide by catalase, the absorption decreases with time. The enzyme activity can be determined from this decrease.

Reagents

1. 0.067M Potassium phosphate buffer (pH7.0)
2. Hydrogen peroxide - Phosphate buffer: Diluted 0.16 ml of H2O2 (10% w/v) to 100 ml phosphate buffer, prepared fresh. The absorbance of the solution should be about 0.5 at 240nm with 1 cm light path.

Procedure

Pipetted into the experimental cuvette 3ml of hydrogen peroxide- phosphate buffer. Mixed in 0.01-0.04ml of plasma with the glass or plastic rod flattened at one end. The cuvettes were read at 240 nm against the control. Noted the time required for a decrease in absorbance from 0.45-0.4. The value was used for calculation. If 't' was greater than 60 seconds, the measurement was repeated with more concentrated solution of the sample. One unit of enzyme activity was defined as µmole of H2O2 decomposed by one enzyme unit of catalase. Calculated the activity and expressed in units per mg protein. One enzyme unit was calculated as the amount of enzyme required to decrease the absorbance at 240nm by 0.05 units.

Appendix - 8
Estimation of Superoxide dismutase activity
Spectrophotometry method
(Beauchamp and Fridovich, 1971)

Principle

Superoxide dismutase uses the photochemical reduction of riboflavin as oxygen generating systems and catalyses the inhibition of Nitro Blue Tetrozolium (NBT) reduction, the extent of which can be assayed spectrophotometrically at600nm.

Reagents

1. 250mM Potassium phosphate buffer (pH7.8)
2. 100mMMethionine
3. 10mMRiboflavin
4. 750µM Nitro Blue Tetrazolium (NBT) salt
5. 5mMEDTA

Procedure

Mixed a 3ml reaction cocktail containing: 50mM potassium phosphate buffer, 13mM methionine, 2µM riboflavin, 0.1mM EDTA and 75µl NBT. To the test 0.1 ml of plasma was added. The reagents were added in dark. Reduced NBT was measured spectrophotomerically at 560nm after exposure to light for 15 minutes. The 50% inhibition of the reaction between riboflavin and NBT in the presence of methionine is taken as 1 unit of SOD activity. The enzyme activity was expressed as units/ml of sample.

Appendix - 9
Estimation of Glutathione peroxidase activity
Spectrophotometry method
(Rotruck et al., 1973)

Reagents

1. 0.4M Sodium phosphate buffer (pH7.0)
2. 10mM Sodiumazide
3. 4mM Reduced glutathione 4. 2.5mMH2O2
5. 10% Trichloro aceticacid
6. Phosphate solution: 0.3mM Disodium hydrogenphosphate
7. DTNB reagent: 40 mg of 5, 5 dithiobis (2-nitro benzoic acid) / 100ml of 1% Sodium citrate
8. Reduced glutathione standard: 20 mg percentsolution.

Procedure

0.4ml of buffer, 0.1ml sodiumazide, 0.2ml reduced glutathione, 0.1ml of plasma,

0.1 ml hydrogen peroxide and water were taken to a final incubation volume of 2.0 ml. The test tubes were incubated at 300C for 10 minutes. The reaction was terminated by the addition of 0.5 ml of trichloroacetic acid. To determine the residual GSH content, 1 ml supernatant was removed by centrifugation and added 3ml of disodium hydrogen phosphate and 1ml of DTNB reagent. The colour was read at 412 nm. A blank was prepared with only di sodium hydrogen phosphate and 1ml of DTNB reagent. Suitable a liquots of the standard were taken and treated similarly. The activity was expressed as μg of glutathione consumed/minute/ml of sample.

Appendix - 10
Estimation of Glutathione -S- transferase activity
Spectrophotometry method
(Habig et al., 1974)

Principle

The enzyme activity is measured by its ability to conjugate glutathione (GSH) and 1- chloro 2,4-dinitrobenzene (CDNB), the extent of conjugation causing a proportionate change in the absorbance at 340nm.

Reagents

1. 1mM 1- Chloro 2, 4-dinitrobenzene (CDNB) inethanol
2. 1mMGlutathione
3. 0.1M Phosphate buffer (pH6.5)

Procedure

The assay was done at 25°C under conditions giving activities linear with respect to incubation time and protein concentration for at least 3 minutes. The enzyme activity was determined by monitoring the change in absorbance at 340nm in a spectrophotometer. 0.1ml of both substrates (GSH and CDNB) were taken and made upto a volume of 2.9ml in 0.1M phosphate buffer at room temperature. The reaction was started by the addition of 0.1ml of plasma to this mixture; the readings were recorded against distilled water blank for a minimum of three minutes. The complete assay mixture without the plasma served as the control to monitor non-specific binding of the substrate. The final concentration of ethanol in the mixture was always less than 4%.

Glutathione-S-transferase activity was expressed as µmoles of CDNB conjugated/minute/ml of sample.

Appendix - 11
Estimation of Vitamin A Spectrophotometry method (Bayfield and Cole, 1980)

Principle

The colour produced by vitamin A, its acetate or palmitate with TCA is proportional in intensity to its concentration, which is measured at 620 nm in a spectrophotometer.

Reagents

All reagents were prepared fresh. Exposure of samples and reagents to light was avoided at all times.

1. Saturated Trichloro acetic acid (TCA) in chloroform: 15 g clear TCA crystals were dissolved in 25 ml of alcohol-free chloroform, stored in dark.
2. Standard vitamin A: 1.5 mg vitamin A palmitate / 10 ml ofchloroform.
3. Petroleum ether(40-60oC)
4. 95% ethanol

Vitamin A extraction

Equal volume of ethanol was added to 0.1 ml plasma and shaken with 0.3 ml petroleum ether for 3minutes. This was centrifuged to separate the layers. Petroleum ether layer was pipetted, evaporated to dryness, dissolved in 0.5ml alcohol-free chloroform and was taken as test.

Procedure

Aliquots of the standard were pipetted out into a series of clean, dry test tubes and 0.2 ml test was taken in another test tube. The volumes in all the tubes were made up to 1.0 ml with chloroform. 2 ml of TCA reagent was added and rapidly mixed with the contents of the tube. The absorbance was recorded immediately at 620 nm in a spectrophotometer. Constructed a standard graph and read off the concentration in the sample.

Appendix - 12
Estimation of Vitamin C Spectrophotometry method
(Omaye et al., 1979)

Principle

Ascorbic acid is oxidised by copper to form dehyroascorbic acid and diketoglutaric acid. These products are treated with 2,4 dinitrophenyl hydrazine to form the derivative of bis 2,4 dinitro phenyl hydrazine. This compound in strong sulphuric acid undergoes a rearrangement to form a product with an absorption band that is measured at 520 nm. The reaction is run in the presence of thiourea to provide a mildly reducing medium which helps to prevent interference from non-ascorbic acidchromogens.

Reagents

1. 5% TCA
2. 65% Sulphuricacid
3. DTCS reagent: 3 g of 2,4 DNPH, 0.4 g thiourea and 0.05 copper sulphate dissolved in 9 N sulphuric acid and made up to 100ml.
4. Standard: Ascorbic acid in the range of 4-20 μg/ml was prepared in 5% oxalic acid.

Procedure

0.1 ml of plasma was precipitated with 5% ice-cold TCA and centrifuged for 20 min. 0.1 ml of the supernatant was mixed with 0.02 ml of DTCS reagent and incubated for 3 hours at 37°C. Then 0.15 ml of ice-cold 65% sulphuric acid was added. Mixed well and the solutions were allowed to stand at room temperature for an additional 30 min. Absorbance was determined at 520 nm. The results were expressed asmg/dl.

Appendix - 13
Determination of Lipid Peroxidation in Serum (Thiobarbituric method - Ledwozyw et al., 1986)

Principle

Melondialdehyde (MDA) produced during peroxidation of lipids served as an index of lipid peroxidation. Malondialdehyde reacts with thiobarbituric acid (TBA) to produce a pink colour product which is measured at 530 nm.

Reagents

1. 10% tricholoro acetic acid: 10g in 100 ml of distilledwater
2. Saline: 0.9% sodiumchloride
3. Thiobarbituric acid (TBA): 500 mg of thiobarbituric acid was dissolved in 6.0 ml of 1 M sodium hydroxide and to the solution 69 ml of distilled water wasadded
4. Stock Standard Malondialdehyde: 0.05 ml of stock solution of 1,1′,3,3′ tetra ethoxy propane bis diethyl acetate (TEP) was made up to 1.0 ml with 0.9% saline and 0.03 ml of 6N hydrochloric acid was added and made up to 100 ml with distilledwater.
5. Working Standard: 1.0 ml of the stock was diluted to 50ml with distilled water to obtain a concentration of 50nmol/ml.

Procedure

Reagent	Blank	S1	S2	S3	S4	S5	Test
Working Standard (µl)	-	100	200	300	400	500	-
Standard Concentration	-	5	10	15	20	25	-
(nmol/ ml)	500	400	300	200	100	-	400
Water(µl)	-	-	-	-	-	-	100
Serum sample(µl)	1.5	1.5	1.5	1.5	1.5	1.5	1.5
Trichloro acetic acid (ml)							
Incubated at room temperature for 15 minutes							
TBA (ml)	1.5	1.5	1.5	1.5	1.5	1.5	1.5
Kept in a boiling water bath for 30 minutes							

Measured the absorbance at 530 nm and the lipid per oxidation was expressed as the amount of nmol of MDA/ ml of serum.

Appendix - 14
Estimation of Vitamin E Spectrophotometry method (Quaife et al., 1949)

Principle

Vitamin E can be estimated using Emmerie-Engel reaction which is based on the reduction of ferric to ferrous ions by tocopherols, which then forms a red colour with 2, 2′-dipyridyl. Tocopherol and carotenes are first extracted with xylene and read at 460nm to measure carotenes. A correction is made for this after adding ferric chloride and read at 520nm.

Reagents

1. Absolutealcohol
2. Xylene
3. 2, 2′- dipyridyl: 1.2 g in 1 litre of N-propanol.
4. Ferric chloride solution: 1.2 g of $FeCl_3 .6H_2O$ in 1 litre of ethanol and kept in a brown bottle.
5. Standard solution: Dissolved 100mg of tocopherol acetate in 1liter absolutealcohol.

Procedure

Into 3 stoppered centrifuge tubes (test, standard and blank) pipetted out 0.3 ml of plasma, 0.3 ml of standard and 0.3 ml of water respectively. Added 1.0 ml ethanol, 1.0 ml xylene to all the test tubes, stoppered, mixed well and centrifuged. Transferred 1.0 ml of xylene layer into another stoppered tube, taking care not to include ethanol layer. Added 1.0 ml of 2, 2′- dipyridyl reagent to each tube, stoppered and mixed. The test and standard were read against the blank at 460nm. Then beginning with the blank, in turn, added 0.33 ml of ferric chloride solution. After 15 minutes the test and standard were read against the blank at 520 nm.

Appendix 15
Estimation of Clara cell protein
Lakind et al., 2007

Principle

The microplate provided in this kit has been pre-coated with an antibody specific to CC16. Standards or samples are then added to the appropriate microplate wells with a biotin-conjugated antibody specific to CC16. Next, Avidin conjugated to Horseradish Peroxidase (HRP) is added to each microplate well and incubated. After TMB substrate solution is added, only those wells that contain CC16, biotin-conjugated antibody and enzyme- conjugated Avidin will exhibit a change in color. The enzyme-substrate reaction is terminated by the addition of sulphuric acid solution and the color change is measured spectrophotometrically at a wavelength of 450nm ± 10nm. The concentration of CC16 in the samples is then determined by comparing the O.D. of the samples to the standardcurve.

Reagents and Materials

Reagents Quantity Reagents Quantity Pre coated, ready to use 96-well strip plate

Plate sealer for 96 wells 4 Standard 2 Standard Diluent

Detection Reagent A 1×120μL Assay Diluent A

Detection Reagent B 1×120μL Assay Diluent B 1×12mL TMB Substrate

Stop Solution 1×6mL Wash Buffer (30 × concentrate)

Cell Lysates - Cells need to be lysed before assaying according to the following directions.

1. Adherent cells should be washed by cold PBS gently, and then detached with trypsin, and collected by centrifugation at 1,000×g for 5 minutes (suspension cells can be collected by centrifugation directly).
2. Wash cells three times in coldPBS.
3. Resuspend cells in fresh lysis buffer with concentration of 107 cells/mL. If it is necessary, the cells could be subjected to ultra sonication till the solution is clarified.
4. Centrifuge at 1,500×g for 10 minutes at 2-8oC to remove cellular debris. Assay immediately or aliquot and store at ≤ - 20oC.

Procedure

1. Determine wells for diluted standard, blank and sample. Prepare 7 wells for standard, 1 well for blank. Add 100µL each of dilutions of standard (read Reagent Preparation), blank and samples into the appropriate wells. Cover with the Plate sealer. Incubate for 1 hour at 37oC.
2. Remove the liquid of each well, don'twash.
3. Add 100µL of Detection Reagent A working solution to each well, cover the wells with the plate sealer an incubate for 1 hour at37oC.
4. Aspirate the solution and wash with 350µL of 1× Wash Solution to each well using a squirt bottle, multi-channel pipette, manifold dispenser or auto washer, and let it sit for 1~2 minutes. Remove the remaining liquid from all wells completely by snapping the plate onto absorbent paper. Totally wash 3 times. After the

last wash, remove any remaining Wash Buffer by aspirating or decanting. Invert the plate and blot it against absorbent paper.

5. Add 100µL of Detection Reagent B working solution to each well, cover the wells with the plate sealer and incubate for 30 minutes at37oC.
6. Repeat the aspiration/wash process for total 5 times as conducted in step4.
7. Add 90µL of Substrate Solution to each well. Cover with a new Plate sealer. Incubate for 10 - 20 minutes at 37oC (Don't exceed 30 minutes). Protect from light. The liquid will turn blue by the addition of Substrate Solution.
8. Add 50µL of Stop Solution to each well. The liquid will turn yellow by the addition of Stop solution. Mix the liquid by tapping the side of the plate. If color change does not appear uniform, gently tap the plate to ensure thorough mixing.
9. Remove any drop of water and fingerprint on the bottom of the plate and confirm there is no bubble on the surface of the liquid. Then, run the micro plate reader and conduct measurement at 450nm immediately.

Appendix 16
Estimation of Leukotriene B4
Montuschi, 2009

Principle

This assay is based on the forward sequential competitive binding technique in which LTB4 present in a sample competes with a fixed amount of horseradish peroxidase (HRP)-labeled LTB4 for sites on a chicken polyclonal antibody. During the incubations, the chicken polyclonal antibody becomes bound to the rabbit anti-chicken antibody coated onto the microplate. Following a wash to remove excess conjugate and unbound sample, a substrate solution is added to the wells to determine the bound enzyme activity. Immediately following color development, the absorbance is read at 450 nm. The intensity of the color is inversely proportional to the concentration of LTB4 in the sample

Reagents

1. Rabbit Anti-chicken Microplate (Part 893074) - 96 well polystyrene microplate (12 strips of 8 wells) coated with a rabbit anti-chicken polyclonal antibody.
2. LTB4 Conjugate (Part 893075) - 6 mL of LTB4 conjugated to horseradish peroxidase with red dye and preservatives.
3. LTB4 Standard (Part 893077) - 25 ng of LTB4 in buffer with preservatives.
4. Lyophilized. Primary Antibody Solution (Part 893076) - 6 mL of a chicken polyclonal antibody to LTB4 in buffer with blue dye and preservatives.

5. Calibrator Diluent RD5-44 - 21 mL of a 25-fold concentrated solution of buffered surfactant with preservatives.
6. Color Reagent A (Part 895000) - 12.5 mL of stabilized hydrogen peroxide.
7. Color Reagent B (Part 895001) - 12.5 mL of stabilized chromogen (tetramethylbenzidine).
8. Stop Solution (Part 895032) - 6 mL of 2 N sulfuric acid. Plate Covers - 4 adhesive strips.

Procedure

1. Prepare all reagents, working standards and samples
2. Remove excess micro plate strips from the plate frame, return them to the foil pouch containing the desiccant pack, reseal.
3. Add 150 µL of Calibrator Diluent RD5-44 to the NSB wells.
4. Add 100 µL of Calibrator Diluent RD5-44 to the zero standard (B0)wells.
5. Add 100 µL of Standard or sample* to the remaining wells.
6. Add 50 µL of the Primary Antibody Solution to each well (excluding the NSB wells). All wells except the NSB wells will now be blue in color. Cover with the adhesive strip provided. Incubate for 1 hour at room temperature on a horizontal orbital microplate shaker (0.12" orbit) set at 500 µ 50rpm.
7. Do not wash the plate. Add 50 µL of LTB4 Conjugate to each well. All wells except the NSB wells will now be violet in color. Cover with a new adhesive strip. Incubate for 2 hours at room temperature on the shaker.

8. Aspirate each well and wash, repeating the process three times for a total of four washes. Wash by filling each well with Wash Buffer (400 µL) using a squirt bottle, manifold dispenser or auto washer. Complete removal of liquid at each step is essential to good performance. After the last wash, remove any remaining Wash Buffer by aspirating or decanting. Invert the plate and blot it against clean paper towels.
9. Add 200 µL of Substrate Solution to each well. Incubate for 30 minutes at room temperature on the benchtop. Protect fromlight.
10. Add 50 µL of Stop Solution to each well. The color in the wells should change from blue to yellow. If the color in the wells is green or the color change does not appear uniform, gently tap the plate to ensure thorough mixing.
11. Determine the optical density of each well within 30 minutes, using a microplate reader set to 450nm

Appendix 17
Estimation of Interleukin 8 (IL-8)
Ware et al., 2009

Materials required

1. Microplate reader with 450 ± 10nm filter. 2. Single or multi-channel pipettes with high precision and disposable tips. 3. Microcentrifuge Tubes. 4. Deionized or distilled water. 5. Absorbent paper for blotting the microplate. 6. Container for Wash Solution. 7. 0.01mol/L (or 1×) Phosphate Buffered Saline(PBS), pH7.0-7.2.

Procedure

1. Determine wells for diluted standard, blank and sample. Prepare 7 wells for standard, 1 well for blank. Add 100μL each of dilutions of standard (read Reagent Preparation), blank and samples into the appropriate wells. Cover with the Plate sealer. Incubate for 1 hour at 37oC.
2. Remove the liquid of each well, don'twash.
3. Add 100μL of Detection Reagent A working solution to each well, cover the wells with the plate sealer and incubate for 1 hour at37oC.
4. Aspirate the solution and wash with 350μL of 1× Wash Solution to each well using a squirt bottle, multi-channel pipette, manifold dispenser or autowasher, and let it sit for 1~2 minutes. Remove the remaining liquid from all wells completely by snapping the plate onto absorbent paper. Totally wash 3 times. After the last wash, remove any remaining Wash Buffer by aspirating or decanting. Invert the plate and blot it against absorbent paper.

5. Add 100µL of Detection Reagent B working solution to each well, cover the wells with the plate sealer and incubate for 30 minutes at37oC.
6. Repeat the aspiration/wash process for total 5 times as conducted in step4.
7. Add 90µL of Substrate Solution to each well. Cover with a new Plate sealer. Incubate for 10 - 20 minutes at 37oC (Don't exceed 30 minutes). Protect from light. The liquid will turn blue by the addition of Substrate Solution.
8. Add 50µL of Stop Solution to each well. The liquid will turn yellow by the addition of Stop solution. Mix the liquid by tapping the side of the plate. If color change does not appear uniform, gently tap the plate to ensure thorough mixing.
9. Remove any drop of water and finger print on the bottom of the plate and confirm there is no bubble on the surface of the liquid. Then, run the micro plate reader and conduct measurement at 450nm immediately

Appendix 18
Estimation of the activity of Myeloperoxidase (MPO)
Shah et al., 2008

Reagent

TNB Reagent/Standard: TNB Reagent/Standard: TNB is easily oxidizable so it needs to be prepared from DTNB Probe as needed. Use the same day as prepared, discard any unused TNB reagent/standard. The amount of DTNB Probe for each well (standard, sample and background control) is 0.5μl. The amount per well of TCEP is 0.5 μl and of Assay Buffer is 49 μl for a total of 50 μl perwell.

MPO Substrate: Aliquot and store at -20°C. Stable for 2 months. Working solution: Add 5 μl MPO Substrate to 300 μl dH2O. Make fresh and discard unused portion.

Stop Mix: Add 200 μl dH2O and dissolve. Aliquot and store at -20°C. Use within two months. MPO Positive Control: Reconstitute the positive control with 100 μl MPO Assay Buffer. Aliquot and store at -20°C. Use within two months.

Procedure

1. Standard Curve Preparation: Add 150, 140, 130, 120, 110 and 100 μl of MPO Assay Buffer into a series of wells. The Standard will be added to the wells (0, 10, 20, 30, 40, 50 μl respectively) at the end of the sample incubation period (see (4)below).
2. Sample Preparation: Homogenize tissue or cells in 4 volumes of MPO Assay Buffer, centrifuge (13,000g, 10 min) to remove insoluble material. Serum samples can be directly diluted in the MPO Assay Buffer. Add 1-50 μl test samples in 96 well plate. For white blood cells, take 2 ml of blood and lyse RBC using RBC Lysis Buffer. Incubate for 10 min. at room temperature.

Centrifuge at 400 x g for 5 min. and remove the supernatant carefully. Wash the pellet with 1 ml 1X PBS. Centrifuge at 400 x g for 5 min, and remove the supernatant carefully. Lyse the pellet using 200 µl MPO Assay Buffer. Keep on ice for 10 min. Centrifuge at 10,000 x g for 10 min. to remove insoluble material. Collect the supernatant. Add 1-10 µl of the WBC lysate into a 96-well plate. Prepare parallel sample well(s) as background control. Adjust the volume of background control and sample wells to 50 µl/well with Assay Buffer. We suggest testing several doses of a sample to ensure the readings are within the standard curve range.

3. Positive Control Preparation: Add 5 - 10 µl of the reconstituted MPO Positive Control to optional Positive Control well(s). Adjust the final volume 50 µl/well with MPO Assay Buffer.
4. Reaction Mix: Mix enough reagents for the number of assays to be performed. For each well, prepare a total 50 µl Reaction Mix: Reaction Mix Sample Background Control Mix 40 µl MPO Assay Buffer 40 µl MPO Assay Buffer 10 µl MPO Substrate 10 µl dH2O Add 50 µl of the Reaction Mix to each well containing the Samples & Positive Control wells. Add 50 µl of the Sample Background Control Mix to the sample background controls. Mix well. Incubate at 25°C for 30 to 120 min. (record this time as T), then add 2 µl Stop Mix to all sample, Standard wells, background control & Positive Control wells and mix. Incubate another 10 min to stop the reaction & add 50 µl TNB Reagent/Standard to each of the sample, sample background control & Positive Control wells. Add 0-10-20-30-40-50 µl TNB

Reagent/Standard (0-10-20- 30-40-50 nmol respectively) to the Standard wells at this time.

5. Measurement: After 5-10 min, read at 412 nm. The Positive Controls and samples will show decreased color proportional to the amount of enzyme present, calculated as ΔA412nm = A sample background - A sample. It is recommended to use the ΔA values which are in the linear range of the Standard Curve.

Appendix 19
Genotoxicity assessment (COMET ASSAY)
Dhawan and Anderson, 2009

Principle

The single cell gel electrophoresis (SCGE)/ comet assay, developed by N.P. Singh, combines the simplicity of biochemical techniques for detecting DNA single strand breaks (frank strand breaks and incomplete excision repair sites), alkali-labile sites and crosslinking with the single cell approach typical of cytogenetic assays.

Materials

- Dimethylsulfoxide (DMSO)
- Qualigens Disodium EDTA
- Ethidium Bromide Histopaque
- Phosphate Buffered Saline (PBS)
- Sodium Chloride (NaCl)
- Sodium Hydroxide (NaOH)
- TritonX-100
- TrizmaBase

Procedure

1. PBS: Dulbecco's PBS - 1 L packet: add 990 mL dH2O, adjust pH to 7.4, q.s. (quantity sufficient) to 1000 mL, store at roomtemperature.
2. Lysing Solution: Ingredients per 1000 mL: 2.5 M NaCl (146.1 gm) 100mMEDTA (37.2 gm) 10 mM Trizma base (1.2gm)

   Add ingredients to about 700 mL dH2O and begin stirring the mixture. Add ~8 gm NaOH and allow the mixture to dissolve (about 20 min). Adjust the pH to

10.0 using concentrated HCl or NaOH. q.s. to 890 mL with dH2O (the Triton X-100 and DMSO will increase the volume to the correct amount), store at room temperature.

3. Final lysing solution: add fresh 1% Triton X-100 and 10% DMSO, and then refrigerate for at least 30 minutes prior to slide addition.

   Electrophoresis Buffer (300 mM NaOH / 1 mM EDTA):

   Prepare from stock solutions: 1. 10 N NaOH (200 g/500 mL dH2O)2. 200 mM EDTA (14.89 g/200 mL dH2O, pH 10)
4. For 1X Buffer (made fresh before each electrophoresis run): per liter, add 30 mL NaOH and 5.0 mL EDTA, q.s. to 1000 mL, mix well. The total volume depends on the gel box capacity. Prior to use, measure the pH of the buffer to ensure >13.
5. Neutralization Buffer: 0.4 M Tris - 48.5 gm added to ~800 mL dH2O, adjust pH to 7.5 with concentrated (>10 M) HCl: q.s. to 1000 mL with dH2O, store at room temperature.
6. Staining Solution: Ethidium Bromide (EtBr; 10X Stock - 20 µg/mL): add 10 mg in 50 mL dH2O, store at room temperature. For 1X stock - mix 1 mL with 9 mLdH2O.

Preparation of Slides for the SCGE/Comet Assay Materials

- Normal Melting Agarose (NMA)
- Low Melting Point Agarose (LMPA)
- Methanol
- Blue Star Microcentrifuge Tubes
- Micropipettor and Tips
- Conventional / Micro gel electrophoresis (MGE) slides

- Coplin jars (opaque)
- Horizontal Gel Electrophoresis Apparatus

Preparation of base slides

1. Prepare 1% (500 mg per 50ml PBS) and 0.5% LMPA (250 mg per 50 ml PBS) and 1.0% NMA (500 mg per 50 ml in Milli Q water). Microwave or heat until near boiling and the agarose dissolves. For LMPA, aliquot 5 mL samples into scintillation vials (or other suitable containers) and refrigerate until needed. When needed, briefly melt agarose inmicrowave
2. or by another appropriate method. Place LMPA vial in a 37°C dry/water bath to cool and stabilize the temperature.
3. Dip the slides in methanol and burn them over a blue flame to remove the machine oil and dust.
4. While NMA agarose is hot, dip conventional slides up to one-third the frosted area and gently remove (2). Wipe underside of slide to remove agarose and lay the slide in a tray on a flat surface to dry. The slides may be air dried or warmed at 500C for quicker drying. Store the slides at room temperature until needed; avoid high humidityconditions.

Electrophoresis of Microgel Slides

The procedure described is for electrophoresis under pH>13 alkaline conditions.

1. After at least 2hour at ~4°C, gently remove slides from the Lysing Solution. Place slides side by side on the horizontal gel box near one end, sliding them as close together as possible.

2. Fill the buffer reservoirs with freshly made pH>13 Electrophoresis Buffer until the liquid level completely covers the slides (avoid bubbles over theagarose).
3. Let slides sit in the alkaline buffer for 20 minutes to allow for unwinding of the DNA and the expression of alkali-labiledamage.
4. Turn on power supply to 24 volts (~0.74 V/cm) and adjust the current to 300 milliamperes by raising or lowering the buffer level. Depending on the purpose of the study and on the extent of migration in control samples, electrophorese the slides for 30minutes.
5. Turn off the power. Gently lift the slides from the buffer and place on a drain tray. Drop wise coat the slides with Neutralization Buffer, let sit for at least 5 minutes. Drain slides and repeat two moretimes.
6. Slides may be stained with 80µL 1X Ethidium Bromide, leave for 5 min and then dipped in chilled distilled water to remove excess stain. The coverslip is then placed over it and the slides are scored immediately or dried before staining as in step7.
7. Drain slides, keep them for 20 min in cold 100% ethanol or cold 100% methanol for dehydration. Air dry the slides and place them in an oven at 500C for 30 min. Store in a dry area.
8. When convenient, rehydrate the slides with chilled distilled water for 30 min and stain with EtBr as in step 6 and cover with a fresh coverslip. Before viewing slides, blot away excess liquid on the back and edges. After scoring, remove coverslip, rinse in100% alcohol to remove stain, let dry, and store for archival purposes ifneeded

www.ingramcontent.com/pod-product-compliance
Ingram Content Group UK Ltd.
Pitfield, Milton Keynes, MK11 3LW, UK
UKHW041348190726
13845UKWH00026B/480

9 789393 737427